HOW TO
BECOME
STRONG ENOUGH
TO LOVE

HOW TO BECOME STRONG ENOUGH TO LOVE

CREATING LOVING RELATIONSHIPS THROUGH THE SIX-STEP PATHWAY OF INNER BONDING

MARGARET PAUL, PH.D.

MEDIA

Published 2022 by Gildan Media LLC
aka G&D Media
www.GandDmedia.com

Front cover design by David Rheinhardt of Pyrographx

Interior design by Meghan Day Healey of Story Horse, LLC

Library of Congress Cataloging-in-Publication Data is available upon request

ISBN: 978-1-7225-0571-4

10 9 8 7 6 5 4 3 2 1

This book is dedicated to my many thousands of clients who gave me the privilege of helping them heal and become strong enough to love.

Acknowledgments

I am deeply grateful for the individuals and couples who have had the courage to do their inner work with me and become strong enough to love. I honor you for having the willingness and tenacity to face your fears in order to heal.

I'm very blessed for my best friend and fellow Golden Girl, Dr. Erika Chopich, the co-creator of Inner Bonding, for her courage to heal and become on incredible role model for loving. I'm also very grateful for her brilliance, creativity, and wisdom in always knowing the answers when I come to her for help.

I am grateful for my agent, Dan Strutzel, of Inspired Productions, for his belief in Inner Bonding and his support for my work, and to G&D Media for your ongoing support in publishing my work.

I'm very grateful for the support I receive for my work from many of the people in the organization I belong to, The Transformational Leadership Council, and particularly for Marci Shimoff mentoring me in bringing Inner Bonding further out into the world. Thank you for your generosity in sharing so much of your knowledge and experience with me.

I feel very blessed by the Inner Bonding Facilitators who have stepped up to the plate to create and teach The Inner Bonding Facilitator Training Program to people from all over the world—Stel Fine, Karen Kral, Michael Barmack, Grace Escaip, Victor Granville, and Winnie Huff. You are all doing a fantastic job!

I'm so very grateful for Inner Bonding. My ongoing practice of Inner Bonding has brought me so much love, peace, joy, fulfillment, and abundant health.

Finally, I am deeply indebted to my Divine guidance, who is always here for me and who writes, creates, and teaches through me. I would not know how to live my life without the love, compassion, comfort, and wisdom of my Divine guidance.

Contents

Preface

When I was a little girl, all I wanted to be when I grew up was a psychologist. Perhaps because I could always deeply feel others' feelings, I was the kid everyone came to for help. I always wanted to help people feel better.

Having grown up as an only child in an angry, lonely household, I had to find many ways to avoid the heartbreak that was a daily part of my childhood. I learned to be a good girl, caretaking others' feelings while ignoring my own. I learned to stay focused in my head, judging myself in order to get myself to do things right, so that I wouldn't have to feel the pain in my heart. I developed an addiction to food to avoid dealing with the loneliness that was a constant part of my life. I learned many ways of trying to get others' love and approval—but no matter how loving I thought I was, I never felt loved back, and the underlying anxiety never went away.

I was such an anxious child that my mother brought me to a child psychiatrist by the time I was five. He told me to tell my mother to stop yelling at me, and I remember thinking, "You're the doctor. You tell her. She isn't going to listen to me." I didn't think he was a very smart doctor, and that's when I decided to be a psychologist. Even at five, I believed I could do a better job than him!

Starting in adolescence, I tried every kind of therapy that was around at the time, and many different therapists. But they did not have the answers for me. In my own work as a marriage and family therapist, I was often discouraged by the results of the traditional psychotherapy that I had been taught in school.

Immersed in my challenging marriage and in parenting our three children, I was searching not only for how to heal the long-term pain I was in, but for how to create a loving relationship. After seventeen years of working as a traditional psychotherapist, my passion became to find the underlying cause of anxiety, depression, addictions, and relationship problems, and discover a self-healing process that would really work.

Thirty-seven years ago, Dr. Erika Chopich and I met and became fast friends. She too was devoted to learning and healing. She had half of the Inner Bonding® process and I had half. When Spirit helped us put it all together, we knew that we had found the gem we were searching for.

Inner Bonding has completely changed my life. The anxiety is gone, replaced by so much joy! I am never discouraged in being able to help others, because I know that if they learn and practice Inner Bonding, they will heal their relationships as well as discovering their own inner peace and joy.

I want to thank my many clients whose composites are in this book. (All names have been changed.) Through understanding their relationship systems through my eyes, you will gain a profound understanding of what is causing many of the personal and relationship problems in your life, and how to heal them.

I send you blessings on your healing journey.

Dr. Margaret Paul

Introduction

It was Marilyn's first counseling session with me, but it didn't take long before tears began streaming down her cheeks. "I am deeply in love," she wept, "and I'm terrified. I'm thirty-seven, and all I've ever wanted is to be married and have children. Now I've met the man of my dreams, but I'm messing it up," she said, reaching a hand up to wipe away her tears. "I thought it would never happen to me. I thought I was doomed to be an old maid. Now things are wonderful. I've never felt this way about anyone, and I don't want to ruin it, but that's exactly what I'm doing! And I can't seem to stop."

"Stop what?" I inquired.

"I can't seem to stop acting like a jerk! As soon as Jeff and I get really close, really intimate, and we're having a great time, I get terrified and pull away. I withdraw into myself, or I say mean things to him. It's like I'm trying to push him away. Jeff is such a sweet man. He really loves me and he tries everything to help me, but he's getting tired of me acting this way. He won't stand for it forever. It sounds crazy, but sometimes I think I should just end the relationship now, since I'm going to ruin it anyway. What's wrong with me? Why am I doing this?"

In the depths of our souls, we all yearn for love and connection with others. That yearning reflects a basic, even biological, human need. Infants, for example, thrive physically only when they feel deeply loved and cherished. As adults, we experience wrenching, soul-level loneliness and heartbreak when we don't have love and meaningful connection in our lives. Yet all too frequently we don't experience a deep level of connection with anyone—not with our parents or siblings, not with a mate, not even with a best friend.

Why are love, connection, and intimacy so elusive? We sit enraptured at movies that depict two people experiencing the delight of falling in love. We thrill at their discovery of each other, their laughter, their uninhibited joy. We love to read stories about deep friendship, about people committed to truly caring about each other over the long haul. And we yearn for these experiences in our own lives.

Yet when you have a chance to have love, the story may be a little different. Many clients have told me exactly what Marilyn did: "I am deeply in love—and I am terrified!"

This is because many people are not strong enough to love: they don't feel safe enough in themselves to risk loving another. Two major fears get in the way and may undermine a wonderful connection with someone:

- Fear of rejection: the loss of another's love through anger, emotional withdrawal, physical withdrawal, or death.
- Fear of engulfment: the loss of self through being controlled, consumed, invaded, suffocated, dominated, and swallowed up by another.

Until these fears are healed and you learn to feel safe inside, you will react defensively whenever they are triggered. Marilyn reacted to her fears by withdrawing or being mean to Jeff so he would pull away from her. You might react in different defensive ways, but the result will be the same: your reactive behavior will trigger your partner's fears of rejection or engulfment. Now both of you are acting out of fear. Together you have created an unsafe relationship space, where love and intimacy will gradually erode.

What do I mean by the term "relationship space"? How is a "relationship space" different from a relationship?

A relationship space is the environment in which the relationship is occurring. It is the energy created by the two people involved. I think of this environment, this relationship space, as an actual entity that both people are responsible for creating. It can be a safe space, which is open, warm, light, and inviting, or it can be an unsafe space, which is tense, cold, unforgiving, and full of fear. The kind of environment in which your relationship takes place is crucial to its success—or failure.

Many people have spent much time in unsafe relationship spaces. In fact, you may have never experienced a safe relationship space, because you have not yet learned to stay open and become strong enough to love when your fears of being rejected, abandoned, engulfed, or controlled are triggered. When these fears are activated, if you focus on who is at fault or who started it, you perpetuate an unsafe relationship space.

Blaming another for your fears—and for your own reactive, unloving behavior coming from your fears—makes the relationship space even more unsafe.

Then you both feel bad, each believing that your pain is the result of the other person's behavior. You might feel victimized, helpless, stuck, and discon-nected from your partner. You desperately want the other person to see what they are doing that (you believe) is causing your pain. You think that if the other person only understands your feelings, they will change, and you exhaust yourself trying to figure out how to make them understand.

Over time, being in an unsafe relationship space creates more and more distance between the people involved. When you have not created a safe space in which to speak your complete, heartfelt truth about yourself, the love between you gradually dies. And the more you hold back your innermost feelings and experiences, the shallower your connection becomes. Your intimacy crumbles.

In friendships, marriages, and work relationships, your joy, aliveness, and creativity get lost as you give up parts of yourself in an attempt to feel safe. In romantic relationships, passion dries up. Superficiality, boredom, fighting, and apathy take its place. You try valiantly to figure out what went wrong. But too often you might ask, "What am I doing wrong?" or "What are you doing wrong?" rather than inquiring into the underlying fears and resulting self-abandoning behaviors that create the unsafe relationship space.

Only when you look at the relationship space will you see what you are each doing to create the unsafe space. The dual fears of losing the other through rejection and losing yourself through being swallowed up by the other are the underlying causes of your self-abandoning, unloving, reactive behavior. These fears and behaviors are deeply rooted. They cannot be healed or overcome by getting someone else's love. On the contrary, you must heal these fears and the false beliefs underlying your self-abandoning behavior before you can share love—giving and receiving it—with each other.

The key to doing this is learning how to create a safe inner space, where you can work with and overcome your false beliefs and your fears of rejection and engulfment. This is a process, not an event. In this book, I will show you how you can use the powerful Six-Step Inner Bonding pathway to create and maintain the inner safety you need so you can become strong enough to love.

Only when you have achieved inner safety can you create a safe relationship space. Marilyn gradually learned to stop attacking or withdrawing from Jeff and take loving care of herself whenever her fears of rejection and engulfment surfaced. She learned to create inner safety when she felt threatened rather than trying to get Jeff to make her feel safe from her fears. She became strong enough to love.

You can do this too. In fact, any two people who are willing to learn to create their own inner sense of safety can also learn to create a safe relationship space, where their intimacy and passion will flourish and their love will endure. Even if only one of you does this powerful work, you can do much to change an unsafe relationship system into a safe one. One person changing changes the entire system.

This book contains many detailed stories of different relationships to illustrate unsafe relationship systems and show how some couples moved from unsafe systems to safe and loving ones. Their names and details about them have been changed, but the dynamics of their relationships are real. My hope for you is that you will identify with their relationships and, through them, learn how to become strong enough to love and create your own safe and loving relationships with partners, family, friends, and coworkers.

1

What Causes an Unsafe Relationship Space?

Let's begin where many people find themselves: in a relationship where their two core fears of rejection and engulfment are continually being triggered and they are each reacting in ways that are causing relationship distress.

Maybe, like Marilyn, you are terrified by true love. You finally find the person your heart has been yearning for, but you start acting in ways that undermine intimacy.

Or maybe you find yourself in a situation like another one of my clients, a well-to-do man in his early thirties. Mark fell madly in love with Jennifer and pursued her with all the considerable charm he could muster. He showered her with expensive gifts and sent her affectionate cards. At first, Jennifer didn't trust Mark's sudden and complete interest in her, but she finally gave in and opened her heart to him. The moment she opened up, however, he closed down. Mark lost interest in Jennifer and decided he had once again picked the wrong person.

Maybe you are in a long-term relationship where you are either fighting a lot of the time or feeling distant, disconnected, and without passion. Or you may find yourselves going along fine until a conflict arises. Then you can't seem to find way to resolve it. You either try to win by getting angry and defensive, or you give in to avoid the other's anger and defensiveness. You love each other, but you realize that resentment is building because of all the unresolved conflicts.

In each of these situations, as in all unsafe relationship spaces, the dual fears of loss of another's love (rejection) and loss of self (engulfment) have been triggered. Where do these fears come from, and why is it hard to recognize them for what they are?

Shame: The Origin of Fear

These fears are hard for most of us to recognize because they take root so early in our development. Relationship spaces, safe or unsafe, exist not just between partners, but in all relationships: parent-child, sibling-sibling, grandparent-grandchild, child-teacher. When we have grown up in unsafe relationship spaces, in which we have experienced rejection, engulfment, or abuse, we may not even be aware when such a space is unsafe. In other words, an unsafe relationship space is the norm for us. It is the air we breathe, the environment we expect to live in.

Many of us have not experienced safe relationship spaces in our lives or seen them in the lives of the people closest to us. Growing up in an unsafe relationship space inevitably leads to developing fears as well as shame. In the fifty-three years that I have been helping people heal, I have rarely met someone who believed that they were fully worthy and lovable. Instead, my clients describe themselves as "inadequate," "not enough," "inferior," "worthless," "not good enough," "flawed," "defective," "unimportant," "bad," or "having something wrong with me." This is shame speaking. These words reveal that the person believes there is something essentially flawed about them. In our society, most of us have some level of shame.

This persistent belief in our inherent unworthiness and unlovability is derived from two sources in childhood. One is external: we experience ourselves as unworthy and unlovable when we are seen and treated that way by our parents, other caregivers, siblings, teachers, or peers. The other source is internal: we believe we are unlovable because we have chosen to draw that conclusion from our early experiences.

Experiencing Ourselves through the Eyes of Others

As small children, most of us do not know our own worth. Some time after we are born, we forget that our essence is pure love and light, created in the image of Divine Love. We forget that we are a spark of the Divine, an individualized expression of the All.

Unless we are highly enlightened little beings who remember our Source, we need to have our divine essence reflected to us by our parents, teachers, religious leaders, or others in authority.

Instead, those authority figures often reflect what is "wrong" with us, often projecting on to us how they feel about themselves. Our parents or other caregivers may withdraw their attention or approval from us to let us know we did something wrong. We may be told we are bad when we make mistakes or don't live up to someone's expectations. We may be told that our parents' feelings and behavior are our fault: "You make me angry," or "You're making me sick." Our parents may shame us in various ways, saying things like, "What's the matter with you? Why can't you do anything right?" They may hit us, giving us the message that what we did means that we are bad (instead of in error) and have to be punished (instead of being understood). They may sexually abuse us, giving us the message that we are objects to be used. If we are sexually used, or we are punished for doing something wrong or bad in our parents' eyes, we may conclude that we are wrong, bad, or unlovable at our core.

This pattern may continue in school, where we may be shamed by teachers for giving wrong answers or making noise. In addition, there may be abuse by our peers, where other children bully us, taking out on us what they are experiencing in their homes from their parents or siblings.

Sadly, there seem to be few ways to grow up in our society without absorbing the belief that our very essence is unworthy and unlovable.

The False Comfort of Internalizing Shame

Did I say *comfort*? What could possibly be comforting about feeling shame? Why would hanging onto shame feel safe? Let me show you how this can happen.

Even as little children, we are creatures of free will. Ultimately, we and we alone decide what we believe. Why, then, do we absorb so many painful beliefs from our parents? Why do we choose to believe in our own unworthiness and unlovability? Why don't we choose instead to recognize that our parents are wounded and unable to love us in the ways we need to be loved?

It may seem far-fetched to believe that children can recognize this truth, yet some do. They decide very early that their parents are unable to be loving, that there is nothing they can do about it, and that it's not their fault. They seek the love they need elsewhere: from the families of friends, from kind teachers, even from animals—anywhere they can. Very early in their lives they give up ever getting love from their parents, and they move on. As a result, they develop far less shame than those of us who keep trying to get the love we need from our wounded parents or caregivers.

Occasionally I work with people like this. They never blamed themselves for their parents' unloving behavior. Many of them survived incredible abuse and moved on to thrive in their work and relationships. I am awed that they have maintained their inherent ability to share their love with others even though they received very little themselves. They often say things like, "I always knew my parents were crazy, and there was nothing I could do about it."

There is a key difference between those of us who absorbed shame (and thus believe in our unlovability) and those who didn't. The people who didn't develop shame as children saw the truth: there was nothing they could do about the way things were. They saw that the situation wasn't going to change: they were powerless to change their parents' behavior. Having accepted this fact, they moved on and took action where they could—over themselves. They took action to find the love they needed elsewhere. However, they were only able to succeed because other sources of love were actually available to them.

The rest of us, which is most of the people on the planet, unconsciously chose (and still choose) not to see the truth about our parents' inability to love us in the ways we needed to be loved. Instead, we decided that it was our fault that we were not being loved. We believed that if we could only figure out the right way to be, we could get what we needed or avoid what we feared. We believed that we could have control over getting the love we needed. This was not true, but deciding to believe this gave us a sense of comfort, no matter how false. In fact, it may have been a life-saving choice. Had we seen the truth (that we could not use our behavior to earn our parents' love, that we were helpless to change them), and if there was no alternative source of love, our despair might have been so great that we might not have survived. Infants and young children can die from feelings of loneliness and helplessness. This is what used to happen to some babies in orphanages: there was no hope of love, and they died of despair. This may be one thing that is occurring when a baby's death is labeled as "failure to thrive."

So, instead of descending into despair, we chose as children to believe that we were not loved because we were inherently unworthy of love: it was our fault. This belief gave us a sense of control: we were no longer helpless. We told ourselves, "If I am not being loved because I am inherently unlovable, then I can hide away my true self, my essence, and develop a self that will make people give me the love I need."

You may still think so. But you can only believe that you have control over getting love by believing that you are causing others to behave unlovingly toward you. And you can only believe this if you believe there is something wrong with you. Hence your attachment to your shame. In order to protect yourself from feelings of loneliness, heartbreak, despair, and helplessness concerning others, you decide you are at fault, and you embrace shame—and with it the belief that you can control how others feel about you and treat you—if only to do things "right" or if you are "perfect".

As small children, you could not manage the incredibly painful feeling of heartbreak at not being loved. You had to find ways to protect against it. Shame, as bad as it feels, it easier to feel than the heartbreak of not being loved. So you turn to it, along with many other addictions that you learned along the way, to protect yourself against feelings you were too small to manage. Having control over not feeling the heartbreak, loneliness, and helplessness concerning others and events becomes your way of life.

Clinging to Control

When your primary intention is to control, your deepest desire is to avoid feeling and taking responsibility for your fear and pain. You have likely learned many forms of behavior to try to control your own feelings as well as the feelings and behavior of others. This is how your wounded self, your ego, begins to develop.

You hide away your true self because you believe that you are inherently flawed. You try to become the person that the external world says you should be. You try to control how people feel about you through externals such as your looks and your performance. You make others responsible for making you feel worthy and lovable, which is what occurred with Cal and Ruby.

Cal and Ruby

Cal, thirty-two, is a financial consultant, and Ruby, twenty-six, is a real estate agent. They met and fell in love very quickly. Both are attractive and had been in numerous relationships. As so often happens, they were both very open when they met, so they felt safe with each other and loved by each other. They had wonderful, passionate sex, and both felt they had found their soul mate.

However, within a few months of meeting, their fears of rejection and engulfment were triggered, and they reverted to their learned controlling ways of handling these fears.

Ruby grew up with a father whose attention to her depended completely upon how she looked. He was obsessed with her being beautiful, and he often made comments such as, "When you grow up, you will find a wealthy man who will take care of you, because you are so beautiful." Her father had no interest in knowing who Ruby was within. In addition, he had affairs and denied them. Both his affairs and his denial caused Ruby much heartache.

Ruby learned to use her physical attractiveness to get through life. As a result, she often felt threatened by other women. What if her boyfriend thought another woman was more beautiful than her? She was constantly jealous with her boyfriends, and she never trusted that they were telling her the truth.

Cal grew up with an angry, engulfing mother who instilled in him the belief that he could not take care of his own emotional well-being. He believed that he needed a woman to feel safe, so he became addicted to women—specifically, to finding the right woman, who would finally fill his emptiness and make him feel safe. When he met Ruby, he thought she was that woman.

But Cal had a habit of looking at attractive women, always looking unconsciously for the next right woman. Soon after he and Ruby became involved, she started reacting to this habit. Instead of wanting to learn about her own fears and taking responsibility for them or discover what was behind Cal's behavior, she just wanted to control him to make him stop looking at other women. She would rage at him, blaming him for her insecure feelings.

Instead of feeling his painful feelings of loneliness and heartache when Ruby got angry at him and wanting to understand her fears, Cal wanted to control Ruby and reacted to her anger with his own anger, defensiveness, and denial—which only enraged her further. Now she became the angry, engulfing mother, while Cal became the unfaithful, dishonest, and rejecting father.

Both Cal and Ruby needed a safe space to heal the wounds of their childhood, but when their fears of engulfment and rejection were triggered, both went into the intent to control instead of the intent to learn and take responsibility for their own feelings. Their safe relationship space eroded further when Ruby began threatening to leave the relationship every time she caught Cal glancing at another woman. Instead of having both feet in the relationship, she now had one foot in and one foot out. As you can imagine, this created a very unsafe relationship space.

Were Cal and Ruby soul mates? Perhaps. But even soul mates cannot maintain their love in an unsafe relationship space. It did not take long for the passion to leave their relationship. In just a few months, the vicious reactive circle of their relationship system eroded their feelings for each other. After four months, they decided they had made a mistake in choosing each other and moved on.

Cal and Ruby did not necessarily make a mistake in whom they chose, but they certainly made mistakes in who they chose to be. What could Cal and Ruby have done differently? You will learn about this in chapter 3.

The essential issue here has to do with control. Those of us who recognized that there was no way to control our parents or caregivers giving us love, and found alternative ways to get it, had no need to see ourselves as unworthy. The rest of us chose to see ourselves as unworthy and unlovable in order to escape our devastating feelings of helplessness, loneliness, and heartbreak. It was easier to try to fix ourselves in order to get the love we needed than to accept that we couldn't control others' feelings and behavior toward us.

Thus, as a child, perhaps you first externally experienced yourself as being somehow unworthy or unlovable. You then picked up the belief and ran with it, internally defining yourself that way.

Over time, we became addicted to controlling others. The more we attempted to behave as someone who was worthy of love (or the more we tried to get the attention we needed by behaving badly), the more addicted we became to these behaviors.

Take Hillary, for example, who consulted with me because her husband threatened to leave her because of her spending addiction. Hillary was obsessed with everything looking "perfect." She continually spent far more than she and her husband had agreed upon for clothing, furniture, and household decorations. Hillary believed that if she, her three daughters, and her house looked perfect, she could control how others felt about her: She could make them love her.

Although Hillary professed a strong belief in a higher power, she spent no time developing a sustaining connection with a personal source of spiritual guidance, which might have convinced her of her inherent worth and lovability. Her whole sense of worth revolved around externals: how she looked, how her children looked, and how her house looked. Controlling how others felt about her was far more important to her than taking responsibility for developing a true sense of her own inherent worth. As a result, she felt deeply alone and lonely, feelings which often exploded into anger toward her husband and children.

How you define your worth takes you either down a spiraling path into negativity and darkness or upward toward ever more love, joy, and peace. Defining yourself externally through looks or performance is a dead end: you can't be 'perfect' all the time. You will eventually age and lose your looks. You may lose your money, your job, your fine house. All externals are temporal. No matter how good you look, how well you perform, how much you give yourself up to others or get angry and blame, you still don't have any control over how others feel about you. Putting your definition of yourself in others' hands is risky business. It continues to foster the dual fears of rejection and engulfment.

The only thing we actually have control over is ourselves: who we choose to be in any given moment. We can heal our fears and create a safe relationship space with others only when we choose to define our worth internally: through eternal qualities such as caring, compassion, kindness, goodness, integrity, honesty, loyalty, and generosity, as well as our individual gifts and talents.

Roland

At fifty-nine, Roland is tall and slender with a full head of silver hair. He consulted with me because he was suffering from extreme stress and anxiety. His doctor had told him that he had to find a way to handle the stress of his business: it was raising his blood pressure to dangerous levels and causing him constant fatigue. Roland owned a large, high-end clothing manufacturing business. Despite his exceptional good looks, high intelligence, and great wealth, he lived in constant fear and anxiety due to the demands of his business. In addition, he was addicted to seeking out beautiful women to make himself feel safe, worthy, and lovable. His entire sense of identity was tied up in his looks, money, sexual attractiveness, and business achievements.

In addition to being a successful businessman, Roland was a generous and caring man. He ran his company with kindness, and his employees loved him. He enjoyed helping people who came to him with their problems. He offered them not only his considerable wisdom and intelligence, but his money as well, often giving large sums to deserving charities. Yet Roland did not value these qualities in himself. If he had, he would not have been racked with anxiety every day. Instead of embracing his obvious internal assets, he spent his days in fear of losing his financial assets.

Eventually, Roland decided to resolve his anxiety by getting out of the business. But when he started to sell his company, it began to fail. Prospective buyers saw his business as unstable because he wanted out. Roland faced an internal crisis as his anxiety—which came directly from defining his worth by his wealth—skyrocketed.

As long as Roland defined himself externally by his wealth (and by the attention from women that it brought him), his resulting fear and anxiety would create a dark energy. Darkness draws darkness, just as light draws light, and when we choose to define ourselves by our temporal, external qualities, we are in constant fear of losing whatever we are attached to externally.

Roland's constant anxiety created a very unsafe inner space. Would he need to lose everything to find himself? Some people in his situation kill themselves as a way out of what they believe is an impossible situation. They never realize that the very challenge they face is the doorway to the truth of who they are.

Fortunately, Roland made some life-affirming decisions. He realized that by making money his god, he was not living in integrity with himself. He realized he was an old soul and wanted to express his love, but his ego, his wounded self, was keeping him locked onto the earthly path of defining himself externally. Once Roland started defining his worth internally, by his caring and compassion, rather than externally, by his money and looks, his anxiety diminished, and his business sold. Roland no longer wakes up anxious. He is awed and delighted that he now wakes up feeling peaceful and joyful. He has created a safe inner space.

How did Roland accomplish this drastic change? After a lifetime of defining himself externally and living accordingly, how did Roland turn things around so completely?

The work of shifting his focus from external definition to internal definition was not accomplished in a moment. It required that Roland be willing to move beyond society's narrow definition of worth. It required that he be willing to embrace a process of healing his fears, and learn how to define himself through his connection with a spiritual source of love and truth.

Roland turned things around in his life because he devoted himself to practicing the powerful Inner Bonding self-healing process presented in this book.

The Illusion of the American Dream

In our society, famous people such as sports stars, models, and movie stars are revered because they look good or perform well. It doesn't matter if they are mean-spirited, hostile, violent, or uncaring. They may get paid huge sums of money to do commercials, not because they are models of loving behavior, but because of how they look or perform and how much money they have. Defining ourselves externally is reinforced daily in the media.

I have worked with many of these famous people, some of whom come to see me because they continue to feel insecure and anxious, no matter how beautiful, rich, and famous they are. They are disillusioned because they put their belief in the American Dream, which goes like this: "When I have the right house, the right partner, lots of money, good looks, and fame, I will have proved my worth, and I will be happy." But inner peace and happiness continue to elude them, and the result of their external success is an internal world of emptiness, depression, and anxiety, as we see in the suicides of some successful famous people. These people may turn to addictive behavior to fill the inner emptiness that results from defining their worth externally. Their addictions enable them to have control over receiving momentary comfort because they do not know how to turn to a spiritual source for deep and enduring comfort and safety.

These people might also turn to medication for their anxiety and depression. Unfortunately, the psychotropic drugs for anxiety and depression have some nasty side effects, such as suicidal and homicidal behavior. This has led to many current suicides as well as to mass murders. In fact, all the mass shooters have been on these drugs, so drugs are obviously not the answer.

From the outside looking in, Gregory is living the American Dream. Gregory, thirty-two, a rugged-looking, handsome, and successful young man, is a professional athlete with a national sports team. He was raised by highly critical parents whose approval and attention were based on his being perfect, both academically and in sports. When he did not live up to his father's expectations, he was beaten.

Gregory has a beautiful wife, Meg, and two bright young sons. Meg and Gregory consulted with me because Meg was thinking of leaving their marriage. In her words, "I am very happy with my life. I love my children and my friends, and I love who I am as a mother, wife, and friend. But Gregory and I have no connection. I love him, but he does not seem to take in my love. He is often angry at me, the children, and himself. It saddens me to see how much he beats himself up, especially after a losing game. He can't seem to let go of trying to get the approval of his parents and others. At this point in his life, his parents do approve of him, yet he doesn't even take that in. I just don't get it. He has everything. Why is he so angry and unhappy?"

Gregory acknowledged that everything Meg said was true. His whole definition of himself was tied to his performance, and he gave himself no leeway. He treated himself exactly as his parents had treated him. If he played a perfect game, he believed that he was worthy—and the media and fans agreed. But his sense of worth vanished the moment he made a mistake. Then he would verbally abuse himself in an attempt to control his future performance, which inevitably led to his feeling bad.

When he and Meg came to see me, Gregory was on a downward spiral in his playing because he was so tense about his performance. By trying to control his performance and how others thought of him, he had completely lost his enjoyment of his sport, his marriage, and his life. He stood to lose everything that mattered to him unless he shifted his intent from control to learning about loving himself, and unless he learned to connect with a personal source of spiritual guidance to guide and support him in this learning process.

Who Defines Your Worth and Lovability Now?

Imagine that your sense of your own lovability and worthiness—or your sense of unworthiness and unlovability—is a small child within you. Imagine that you have the option of either defining the worth of this child or handing over this responsibility to others.

Imagine that this child is an actual child: your son or daughter, who is exactly like you. If this were your actual child, would you constantly hand over this child to others to define? Would you keep asking others, "Is my child worthy? Is my child lovable? Is my child worth my love?" Would you always be on the lookout for someone to adopt your child so the child would finally feel loved and safe? Would you make others responsible for your child's sense of self-worth and feelings of safety?

Of course, if you didn't want the child, this might be exactly what you would do. But if you wanted to be a loving parent, you would never keep trying to hand your son or daughter over to others to adopt and define. You would accept the responsibility of learning to be a loving parent.

Yet most of us spend a great deal of energy handing our inner child over for "adoption." The moment we are around others, we look to them for a reflection of ourselves. If they don't like us, we decide we are unworthy or unlovable. If they like us, we feel good for the moment. But in the next moment, we have to continue to prove our worth so we can get the approval we so desperately need. In effect, we make others responsible for defining our lovability and worth. This self-abandonment creates a very unsafe inner space.

The moment you hand over the job of defining your worth to others, you create an internal black hole, a void that endlessly needs to be refilled—by others, of course. People who are constantly pulling on others to get their needs filled are an energy drain. Whether you pull with anger, silence, self-pity, incessant talking, complaining, people pleasing, or flattery—any behavior that seeks to control getting attention, approval, sex, and so on—the person on the other end will likely feel drained. Any attempt to get others to fill your emptiness and define your worth creates an unsafe relationship space.

In addition, when you hand over to others the responsibility for defining your worth, and they do not define you the way you want to be defined, you feel victimized, abandoned, and unsafe. Your sense of self is dangling out there, hoping someone will love you enough to make you feel lovable and worthy. This is a truly unsafe way to live. It is giving your essential power to others. Yet is it not others who are abandoning you and making you feeling unsafe: it is *you*.

Only when you accept the responsibility of defining yourself can you move out of victimization and feelings of abandonment and into personal power and emotional freedom. You cannot create a safe inner or relationship space when you abandon yourself and then see yourself as a victim.

You can only stay in a victim position and maintain your illusion of control over others by continuing to believe that you cause others to reject you because of your unworthiness. To do this, you have to maintain your attachment to your shame—your belief that you are inadequate and unworthy in your very essence. What a price to pay for the illusion of having control over others!

Yet the moment you are willing to accept your helplessness in determining whether others love or reject you, and learn how to manage the feelings of loneliness, heartache, and heartbreak over others' unloving behavior, you will let go of shame.

When you define yourself externally, like Hillary, Roland, and Gregory, your intent is to control. Your deepest desire is to find your sense of safety externally, through attention, approval, sex, substances, possessions, and activities. You desperately try to control others into accepting you so that you can feel safe, worthy, and loved. You may also try to control your own feelings through substance and process addictions.

These addictive strategies may seem to work for a while, but the moment your fears of rejection and engulfment are activated, you retreat further into the controlling behaviors of your wounded self: you attack, blame, defend, demand, explain, deny, teach, judge, criticize, shut down, withdraw, resist, comply, give in, lie, become overly nice, and so on. Moreover, when you act out in habitual, controlling ways, your behavior may trigger your partner's or another's fears of rejection or engulfment. They will then react with their own controlling behavior, creating a vicious circle. This is the ultimate unsafe relationship space.

To sum it up, all the ways by which you try to control your own feelings—with substance and process addictions—create an unsafe inner space. Furthermore, all the ways by which you try to control another's feelings about you and behavior toward you create an unsafe relationship space.

Why, in the face of so much suffering, do most people refuse to take responsibility for themselves? The twofold dilemma is that in order to take responsibility, first, we have to surrender our desire to control others (and this is the last thing that the ego, our wounded self, wants to do), and second, we need to be willing to feel and learn to lovingly manage the painful feelings of life that we are avoiding: loneliness, heartache, heartbreak, grief, sorrow, and helplessness concerning others.

Think about all the ways you try to control not feeling your pain. Think also about how you try to control the way others feel about you, the outcomes of things, and your feeling of safety in the external world. Who would you be if you didn't spend your time and energy trying to control these things?

Beyond Looks and Performance

Pretend for a moment that you are great friends with a blind man who cannot see how you look or what you achieve—who relates instead to who you are. What would this man value about you? Would he value your caring, your kindness, your empathy, your understanding, your acceptance, your compassion, your unconditional love? Would he value your gentle voice, your tender touch, your patience with his slower pace when he walked? Would he value your honesty, your integrity, your curiosity, your sense of humor, your laughter? Are these qualities that you value and have embraced within yourself? Would he experience these qualities, or are they hidden away within you?

All of these qualities are fully available to each of us if this is who we desire to be. If you look honestly at yourself, do you value these qualities more than your looks, your achievements, or your money? Or do you value your external assets more than your inner assets?

You might have other wonderful qualities within your essential self that your friend the blind man would also value—natural, God-given talents, such as a beautiful singing voice, the ability to play a musical instrument, a healing touch, or creativity with food.

It is wonderful when we offer our gifts in love, but when we offer them as a way to establish our worth, they may not be fully appreciated. You could make beautiful music or cook your blind friend a wonderful meal, but if your energy with him was needy or dark, he would not feel cared for. Even your innate talents would not be as valuable to him as your kindness and compassion.

Giving Up the Illusion of Control

Carley was raised in a very unusual household. Both of her parents had embarked on paths toward consciousness in their early twenties, even before meeting each other. By the time they had children, they had both had developed a strong sense of their own worth and lovability.

Because they had healed their own shame, they were able to see that the core of Carley was love, peace, and joy. They were able to experience the beauty of her soul and to love her, as well as themselves, unconditionally. It is not that Carley grew up with no shaming. She experienced plenty of rejection from teachers and peers, which her parents helped her to see was not about her personally but about the wounds of those who rejected her. Because her parents were role models for taking responsibility for their own feelings of worth, pain, and joy, Carley naturally learned to do this as well. Because she was not shamed by the people most important to her, she didn't absorb false beliefs about her own core self.

Because she didn't need to control how others saw her (since she knew her own worth), she didn't need shame to maintain an illusion of control over others.

The truth is, I've never met someone like Carley. I had to make her up. She is how I believe we would be if we had grown up with parents who took responsibility for their own feelings and for defining their own worth. This is how I believe our children would be if we did our own inner work before having them.

The vast majority of us did not grow up like Carley. Because we did not receive the love or the loving role modeling we needed, we chose to believe in our shame, and we now use it to maintain the illusion that we have control over getting the love we need. Our wounded self wants to maintain that illusion more than anything. But to maintain the illusion of control, it has to maintain the illusion of our shame coming from the false belief that there is something wrong with us. If we accept that others are independent individuals with the free will to choose to be loving or unloving, accepting or judgmental, we have to accept that we do not cause them to be loving or unloving, accepting or judgmental. We have to acknowledge our lack of control over them. We have to stop saying to ourselves, "What did I do wrong, or what's wrong with me that caused the other person to be angry (or judgmental, or rejecting)?" Yet giving up the illusion of control is the hardest thing for us to do because the whole identity of our wounded self is based on control, and we think our wounded self is who we really are.

In order to give up trying to control others into loving us and defining us, we need to accept and manage our feelings of loneliness, heartache, heartbreak, sorrow, and helplessness over others when they are closed and unloving with us. As long as our intent is to avoid these feelings, we will be unwilling to give up our illusion of control, and as long as we are devoted to trying to control, we cannot become strong enough to love. We cannot create a safe inner space or a safe relationship space while remaining addicted to control.

Beyond Illusion: Accepting the Truth about Control

Our fears of helplessness over others and the outcomes of things lead us to attach meaning to many situations in an effort to feel safe. We look for "signs" that things will come out the way we want. We might develop superstitions in the hope of controlling outcomes, such as, "If I don't walk under a ladder, or step on a crack, or have a black cat cross my path, bad things won't happen." Some people develop elaborate rituals before leaving their home or going to sleep in order to give themselves a sense of control.

One of the relaxing things I sometimes do at night before going to sleep is play computer games in bed on my laptop. Years ago, when I started doing this, I found myself getting more and more tense instead of more relaxed as I played. Then I realized that I was telling myself that if I won this game, it meant that such and such good thing would happen, and if I lost, the thing I wanted to happen would not happen. Winning the game was a "sign," a superstitious way of having control over an outcome. Of course, when I won, I felt reassured, but when I lost I felt anxious. Pretty soon the fun of playing was gone. When I realized that I was doing this, I was able to let go of attaching outcomes to winning or losing, and the fun and relaxation came back into my playing.

How often do you tell yourself that if you had just said or done the "right" thing, things would have turned out differently?

Abigail, in her mid-forties, was heartbroken because her boyfriend of eighteen months had broken up with her. She was ready to settle down after having been single for many years following her divorce, and had been hoping that Arnold was the one. He had said many times that he loved her and wanted to marry her. They had great times together when things were going well, and she could not understand why he was so ready to let all the love and good times go so easily. It seemed as if one minute he was professing his love and his desire to spend his life with her, and the next minute he was gone.

Abigail had learned early in life to cope with her anxiety by telling others what to do. When fear arose in her relationship with Arnold—primarily fear for his well-being and fear about his love for her—she would badger him to do what she felt was best for him. Her energy at these times was frantic and inva-sive. But Abigail was also very open to learning about this behavior and changing it. When it was pointed out to her with caring rather than judgment, she would stop and examine it. The more she examined her behavior, the less she engaged in it, and often weeks would go by before she did it again. Yet it was not a fully healed issue. She was still working on it and had asked Arnold to help her with it.

Arnold was raised by highly invasive and reject-ing parents, and was terrified of being controlled or rejected by others. He had not done the inner work necessary to keep him from taking others' rejection personally or to care for himself in the face of their invasive and controlling behavior. Nor had he devel-oped a powerful loving inner adult who could create a safe inner space. So when Arnold felt invaded, instead of just pointing it out to Abigail and car-ing about the fear behind her invasive behavior, he would get angry and withdraw. In addition, he would tell Abigail that his anger and withdrawal were her fault because she was so invasive.

Arnold was unwilling to do the inner work nec-essary to develop a strong, loving inner adult and become strong enough to love. As long as Abigail was "perfect" and did not act out with her controlling behavior, things between them were fine, but as soon as her fear was triggered and she became invasive, Arnold would act out his own controlling behavior. Abigail was willing to continue to work on herself, but

Arnold apparently was not, so he ended the relationship.

Abigail did not want to accept that she did not cause Arnold to get angry and withdraw: this was what he had learned to do as a child. "If only I had healed faster, if only I had been more aware, if only I had not been such a bitch, we would still be together," she said.

It was not easy for Abigail to see that her "bitchy" behavior was not the cause of Arnold's leaving. Rather, it was his own unwillingness to persevere and learn from the difficult times. All relationships have conflict, and unless both people are committed to staying through them, no relationship will last or remain loving and passionate. Abigail had a hard time accepting that she had no control over Arnold's decision to withdraw and avoid rather than to learn and grow. It was far easier to take his behavior personally than to accept her helplessness over his decision.

I helped Abigail to see that in reality Arnold left, not because of her invasive advice, but because they had grown particularly close and intimate. Their closeness triggered Arnold's fears of rejection and engulfment. As surely as day follows night, Arnold would have found another reason to leave Abigail if she had healed her addiction to giving advice. There was nothing she could do about this. No matter how perfect she was, Arnold's fears and his unwillingness to take responsibility for them and heal them would cause him to leave her.

Accepting this did not lessen Abigail's grief over her loss, but it did lessen her suffering. Suffering occurs when we operate out of false beliefs. Grief is the natural sadness that occurs over loss.

We all have many levels of control issues that come up in relationships. If you observe yourself, you will see how often you tell yourself that "if I do this, he (or she) will do that." For example:

- "If I cry, he will care about me."
- "If I explain, she will see the error of her ways and change."
- "If I withdraw to punish her, she will want to make love to me."
- "If I make love to him, he will connect with me."
- "If I buy her an expensive present, she will be turned on to me."
- "If I give in to my children, they will love me."
- "If I get sick, he will see how he is hurting me."
- "If I am perfect, people will love me."
- "If I keep my mouth shut and no one notices me, I will be safe."

And so on. We just don't want to accept that although we may influence others at times, we have no control over their intent to be open or closed, loving or unloving, accepting or judgmental.

While you have no control over others, you do have total control over yourself and your own intent. In every moment, you can choose the illusion of external safety by attempting to control others and your own feelings, or you can choose internal safety by learning to be loving to yourself and others. In each moment you choose what is most important to you: to control or to learn about loving.

2

Becoming Strong Enough to Love

Behind most of our actions is an intention, whether conscious or not, and so our behavior is generally based on our intent. Just as we can define ourselves in only one of two ways, externally or internally, we can choose to live our lives, in any given moment, in only one of two intents: we can choose the intent to control, avoid, and protect against pain, or we can choose the intent to learn about loving ourselves and others.

We examined the intent to control in chapter 1. We saw how our need to control is tied to core shame and letting others define our worth. We saw that our fears of being rejected and engulfed, and of feeling lonely, heartbroken, and helpless, all fuel our desire to control.

What if we approached life with the intention to learn instead of to control?

Having the intent to learn means that your deepest desire in the moment is to learn about loving yourself and others, even in the face of fear and pain. You are willing to face your fears and feel your painful wounded emotions—the emotions that come from the self-abandonment of your wounded self, such as anxiety, depression, guilt, shame, anger, aloneness, emptiness, and jealousy—in order to learn how you are creating them with your thoughts and behavior and what loving actions you need to take on your own behalf to relieve your pain and bring peace and joy. You are willing to feel your core existential painful feelings, such as loneliness, heartache, heartbreak, grief, and helplessness over others, so that you can nurture them and learn what they are telling you about others and events. When your intent is to learn, your deepest desire is to create inner peace and joy and an inner sense of safety and worth through being kind and loving to yourself and to others. You are focused on supporting your highest good and the highest good of all rather than on controlling and avoiding.

When you are open to learning, you are willing to stop defining yourself by externals and learn to value yourself for your internal qualities. You are willing to reexamine what you were taught about your self-worth as a child. You are willing to learn a new way to view yourself and the world.

Defining Your Essential Self through Spiritual Eyes

When you are open to learning, you are willing to discover who you really are—your essential, true soul self—your inner child. Everything in life changes when you claim your right to define your own worth and lovability. This creates a safe inner space.

Defining your essential soul self is not something you can do from your own limited ego wounded mind. At this level, your mind is programmed—filled with the false, self-limiting beliefs of your wounded self. This self, housed in the lower part of your left brain, called the amygdala, learned to see you through the eyes of your parents, your teachers, your peers, and your siblings. These people may have projected onto you their own core shame: their belief in their own unworthiness and unlovability. Nor may you be able to see the shining truth of your essential self through the eyes of your current peers, because they too may be seeing you through their own wounded, conditioned, filtered lenses.

If the truth about who you are cannot come from your own mind or from the people around you, where are you going to get it? Will looking into a mirror and repeating affirmations, such as "You are a wonderful, beautiful child of God," really show you the worth of your essential self? Many people have tried affirmations without real, long-lasting success. Just being told to love yourself doesn't work either.

The truth needs to come from your spiritual guidance. Only your own higher power has the authority to define you, because only it knows the truth about who you are. No human being on the planet can see into your essence the way your spiritual guidance can. In this chapter, you will learn how to begin accessing this guidance.

Imagine what your life would be like if you knew, with your whole being, that there was nothing wrong with you. Imagine what your life would be like if you never took others' behavior personally, and if you never had to do anything to feel lovable and worthy.

What if you never had to prove that you were a good and caring person or that you had to earn the right to be loved? Imagine what life would be like if you believed you had the right—and the responsibility—to define your worth and bring yourself joy. Imagine the freedom you would feel if your sense of who you are was completely unattached to what anyone else thinks of you.

Let's go further. Imagine the joy of working, loving, and creating as an expression of your very essence rather than as a way to prove your worth. Imagine that your doing comes from your deep inner sense of being rather than from an attempt to define your being. Imagine doing things well for the joy of expressing your soul rather than to get approval.

All of this is possible, and much more accessible than you think. You achieve it by learning how to experience your true worth through spiritual eyes of love and taking loving actions based on the truth of who you really are.

You do not need to come from a particular religious or spiritual background to access the truth about yourself. You do not need to learn any particular form of meditation. You even don't need to believe in God or a Higher Power. But you do need to have a deep desire to define yourself instead of handing over that responsibility to others. You need a deep desire to learn about loving yourself and creating a safe inner space. Your deepest desire determines the outcome of your efforts. If your deepest intention is to control how others define you and get them to give you what you want, you will not learn how to access the truth for yourself, and you will not be able to create either a safe inner space or a safe relationship space. When your deepest desire is to learn to be a loving, compassionate human being, first with yourself and then with others, the journey to healing will open before you.

The journey to healing begins with the six steps of Inner Bonding. Before we go through those steps, think for a moment about what creates a feeling of safety for a child.

Creating Inner Safety

When we were children, what did we really need from our parents or caregivers in order to feel safe? We needed

- To be seen and valued for who we are, and to have our feelings listen to with caring and curiosity.

- To feel that their caring was consistent and reliable.
- To feel that they would protect us from harm.
- To be told the truth and to have promises fulfilled.
- To have them speak up for us when we could not speak up for ourselves.
- To have appropriate yet loving limits and appropriate consequences for unacceptable behavior.
- To have them be role models of loving self-care.
- To have them really see us and hold up a mirror of our shining essence.
- To have their help in learning not to take others' unloving behavior personally.
- To have them provide us ample opportunity to express our talents and passions.
- To be given love that was not conditional, based upon our looks or performance, but unconditional and based upon on our beautiful essence and our devotion to making effort.
- To have them operate from compassion and understanding (love) rather than criticism and judgment (control).

What we need now to feel inner safety is no different. And we can meet these needs by creating a strong, loving inner adult who will act as a loving parent to the child within us, who fears both rejection and engulfment. We need:

- To become strong enough to compassionately embrace our core painful feelings rather than trying to control them with substance and process addictions or blaming others.

- To be open to learning about how we are treating ourselves and what we are telling ourselves that is causing our wounded feelings.

- To develop a loving adult self who is strong enough to handle rejection without taking it personally.

- To become strong enough to know that we will survive—and eventually thrive—if we lose a loved one.

- To become strong enough to take loving care of ourselves when someone tries to control us, even if it means losing that person.

- To become strong enough to speak our truth without blame or judgment, risking disapproval or the loss of another person rather than the loss of our self.

- To become strong enough to stay open-hearted and open to learning, even in the face of others' anger, blame, or attack.

- To become strong enough to disengage from other's attack and blame when disengaging is loving to ourselves.

- To become strong enough to set inner limits against indulging in self-destructive thoughts and behaviors, such as self-criticism, imagining bad things happening, eating badly, smoking, drinking, overspending, or turning into a couch potato.

Developing this strong inner parent, this powerful and loving adult self, is what the six steps of Inner Bonding are about. It takes time and practice, but the process itself is highly rewarding—and so are the results. A person who is devoted to practicing Inner Bonding will always be able to create a strong, loving inner adult.

Beginning the Six Steps of Inner Bonding

Think for a moment about what seems most important to you in any given moment: controlling or learning. Most people believe that they generally have their own highest good and the highest good of others in mind. Many are unlikely to admit that the most important thing to them is to control how others feel about them or avoid responsibility for their own feelings by indulging in substance or process addictions.

Often there is a big difference between a person's true desire and the desire they think they have. This is the difference between our conscious desire and our subconscious desire. Consciously, of course, most of us desire to support the highest good of all, but subconsciously, in the fearful, wounded part of ourselves, not only do we want control over others and the outcome of things, but we believe we can have this control. Our subconscious desire governs our actions, regardless of what we consciously think we want. This means that by making the subconscious conscious, we give ourselves the power to change our intent and make new choices.

Your intent is whatever is most important to you—your primary motive, your highest priority, your main goal, your deepest desire—in any given moment. Your intent governs how you think, feel, and behave. It is a powerful and creative force, the very essence of free will. A major aspect of Inner Bonding is becoming aware of whether your intent in any given moment is to learn or to control.

How do you discover your intent? Your emotions, in any given moment, reflect your intent. If you are currently feeling safe, content, and peaceful inside (without alcohol, marijuana, or other drugs, or from the momentary good feelings of getting others' attention or approval), then you are likely open to learning about what is loving to yourself, and you are being loving to yourself. If you are currently feeling sorrow, heartache, heartbreak, loneliness, or grief, but you still feel safe and peaceful inside (yes, it is possible), then you are showing up as a loving adult for your own feelings, and your intent is to be loving to yourself.

If you are currently feeling anxious, depressed, guilty, shamed, angry, hurt, resentful, jealous, insecure, empty, alone, or numb, you have abandoned yourself in some way. These emotions indicate that your intent is to avoid responsibility for your own feelings through some form of controlling or avoidant behavior.

Obviously, it is difficult to know your intent if you stay in your head rather than in your body—in your mind rather than your feelings. Many people have spent years avoiding their emotions by not being present in their bodies in the moment.

For this reason, it is a big challenge for many people to become aware of their true intent in the moment. Right now, take a few minutes to go inside and become aware of your emotions in this moment. Move your focus out of your mind and into your body, breathing into your body and noticing any physical sensations that indicate tension or peacefulness.

Based on what you feel, now notice your intent— to avoid and control, or to learn about love.

When our intent is to learn, what are we wanting to learn about? One of the main things is the beliefs and behavior of our wounded self.

Who Is the Wounded Self?

Try to imagine that inside you are a number of different parts. We often hear ourselves say things like, "A part of me wants this, but a part of me wants that," or "A part of me feels this way, but a part of me feels that way." For example, "A part of me wants to go to work, but a part of me wants to stay in bed." "A part of me wants to exercise, but a part of me would rather just watch TV." "A part of me wants to make love, but a part of me is too tired." "A part of me really wants to lose weight, but a part of me eats everything in sight."

Imagine that these parts are a family of children of different ages. Perhaps there is a wounded little baby part that wasn't held enough and yearns for this holding. Maybe there is a wounded three-year-old part that got very frightened when Mom and Dad were fighting and learned to shut down and tune things out. There might be a wounded elementary-school age part that was bullied or left out and is terrified of rejection, and another young part who felt invaded and controlled by Mom and Dad. Perhaps one part was physically abused and is terrified of doing anything wrong, believing that being perfect will protect you against others' anger. Another part may have been sexually abused and now uses sex to get attention—or just the opposite: making you gain a lot of weight to feel safe. Maybe there is a wounded adolescent part who rebelled against being controlled and is resistant to everything. There may be a part who learned to judge yourself as a way to feel safe by trying to have control over doing things right. All of us have one or more of these different parts, and they make up our wounded self.

Whenever a wounded part of us is in charge, our intent is to control and avoid pain. Our wounded parts want nothing more than to control how people feel about us. These parts' job is to control getting love, attention, or approval and to use addictions to suppress our feelings of loneliness, heartache, heartbreak, and helplessness when we are not getting the love we need.

Perhaps one of these wounded parts is usually in charge of your life. Let's say that an adolescent part is in charge of keeping you safe from being controlled by others and from feeling the pain of rejection. Perhaps as an actual adolescent you attempted to stay safe by

- Resisting everything
- Giving in and pleasing people
- Shutting down and withdrawing in the face of fear or pain
- Getting angry and blaming others
- Explaining and defending
- Being self-critical or critical of others
- Eating, drinking, or using drugs
- Spacing out in front of the TV
- Endless hours of computer games
- Spending money
- Having sex
- Masturbation with Internet porn
- Gambling

While growing up, you might have discovered dozens of ways to try to control getting love and avoiding pain. All of these protective, controlling behaviors come from your wounded self, with its intent to control.

None of your controlling behaviors will ever make you strong enough to love. None of them will create the kind of inner safety that will enable you to risk being open and vulnerable enough to deeply love another. Nor will they create a safe enough inner space for your core soul self to emerge with all of its aliveness, creativity, joy, passion, and sense of purpose. Your soul self may be hidden away somewhere because your wounded self believes that your essence is bad, wrong, flawed, shameful, or a burden to be borne. Your wounded self may have concluded that it was your fault that you were being treated badly and not getting the love you needed. Your core self, your incredible essence and unique individual expression of Spirit, might be hidden so deep that you have no idea how magnificent you really are.

When a wounded part of you is in charge of creating safety, all you can hope for is a momentary feeling of safety. This is the fleeting feeling of relief that comes from eating chocolate when you are anxious. The chocolate—or alcohol, sex, anger, withdrawal, or resistance—may help you dull the pain of rejection, but it will never help you learn to be a strong, loving adult who

- Does not take rejection personally.
- Sets loving limits against engulfment by others.
- Has the courage to speak your truth without blame or judgment.
- Experiences grief and heartbreak (but not the suffering of self-abandonment) in the face of loss.
- Stays open to learning in the face of fear.
- Takes loving action on your own behalf and on behalf of others.
- Manages loneliness, heartache, heartbreak, sorrow, and helplessness in loving, compassionate ways.

Does this mean that in order to become strong enough to love, we need to get rid of our wounded parts? No. Just as we do not get rid of angry or withdrawn children, we do not get rid of difficult parts of ourselves. They need to be healed, and, like actual children, they are healed by love—in this case, the love of a compassionate inner adult. As we develop our loving adult self, our wounded parts feel safe enough to let go of control, and the energy they have been spending to withstand their fears and pain is channeled back to fuel the creativity and spontaneity of the core self.

Only a powerful inner adult can create the deep sense of inner safety we all need and desire. Only a loving inner adult with an intent to learn can take loving care of all of our difficult emotions—both the natural emotions resulting from painful life experiences and those resulting from the thoughts, beliefs, and behavior of the wounded self.

You might want to lump these different emotions together and call them your *inner child*. Envisioning your emotions as your inner child may make it easier to remember that you are responsible for taking care of your own feelings.

Your Inner Guidance System

Your inner child—your feeling self—is your inner guidance system, letting you know each moment whether or not your thoughts and behavior are in alignment with your highest good.

Your good feelings of love, peace, joy, content-ment, fulfillment, passion, aliveness, and vitality are letting you know that your thoughts and behavior are in alignment with who you really are—that you are going the right way on the freeway of life. Your posi-tive emotions are letting you know that you are taking loving care of yourself in your thoughts and actions.

Your painful core feelings of loneliness, heartache, heartbreak, sorrow, grief, helplessness concerning others, outrage over injustice, and fear of real and present danger are letting you know that someone is being unloving, that painful things are happening externally, or that someone or something is danger-ous. These feelings are giving you information about what is happening externally so that you can take lov-ing action.

Your painful wounded feelings of fear, anxiety, depression, guilt, shame, anger, jealousy, aloneness, emptiness, and so on are letting you know what is happening internally—that your thoughts and behav-ior are off the mark, out of kilter, out of alignment with who you are and what is in your highest good. You are going the wrong way on the freeway, against the flow of traffic, and creating big problems for yourself. These painful feelings are letting you know that you have abandoned yourself in your thoughts and actions.

Self-abandonment occurs in four major ways:

- Ignoring your feelings by staying focused in your mind rather than in your body, where your feel-ings are.

- Judging yourself or telling yourself lies such as, "I'm such a jerk. I can never do anything right," or "I'm so fat and ugly. No one will ever love me," or "I'm a loser," or "I can control how others feel about me by being perfect." These lies will always create anxiety and stress, and these feelings are letting you know that you are abandoning yourself.

- Turning to addictions to numb your feelings. If you are feeling loneliness, heartache, heartbreak, grief, or helplessness over others, and you are ignoring these feelings by focusing in your mind rather than your heart, your inner child will feel abandoned and alone. If you are feeling angry, anxious, or depressed, and you ignore these feelings by turning to addictions, your inner child not only will feel abandoned but will feel even more angry, anxious or depressed. These feelings are your inner child's way of letting you know that you are off the mark in your thinking and behavior. When you then numb your feelings with addictions, you are creating even more pain and suffering.

- Handing your inner child to others to define your worth and lovability. You are essentially saying to your inner child, "I don't think you are worthy enough of my love and care. You are a burden to me, so I have to find someone else to love you and care for you." Handing your inner child to others for attention and approval creates the wounded emotions that are your inner child's way of letting you are rejecting and abandoning yourself.

Once again, take a moment to breathe deeply, follow your breath, and go inside. Focus on what you are feeling in your body. Notice the physical sensations: is there any tightness, fluttering, heaviness, hollowness? What emotion would you ascribe to these physical sensations? Anxiety, sadness, loneliness, peacefulness, excitement, fear, anger?

Now notice what you want to do with any difficult feelings you are experiencing. Do you want to avoid or suppress them by using some substance or doing some activity? Or are you open to embracing your emotions and learning how to take loving care of these feelings, which are your inner child—your inner guidance system? Are you curious about what you might be thinking, believing, or doing that is causing your painful wounded emotions?

If you want to avoid or suppress your emotions, your intent in this moment is to control. At this point, you are shutting yourself off from your inner guidance system, which will always result in even more pain. If you want to learn what would be loving to yourself and how you might be causing these feelings through self-abandonment, your intent in this moment is to learn.

An intent to control does not make you bad or wrong. In fact, in order to discern your true intent, you need to avoid judging your intent to control. You need to look at discovering your controlling behavior in the same way you would look at a treasure hunt. Just as discovering a great treasure gives you new options in life, discovering your controlling behavior gives you the awareness you need to make new choices. So instead of shaming yourself when you discern your intent to control, welcome the information and be open to learning about your controlling behavior.

The Secrets to Becoming an Inner Loving Adult

We are operating as loving adults when our intent is to learn about loving ourselves and we are taking loving action. We are being loving adults when we are compassionate—kind, tender, gentle, caring, and understanding—rather than judgmental with ourselves and others, and we take actions that support our highest good and the highest good of all.

As I've previously stated, most of us have had no adequate role models for being loving adults, since most of us had parents who did not know how to take loving care of themselves. So what is the secret to learning about what is loving to ourselves? How do we do it? By connecting to and communicating with a role model that is of a spiritual nature.

You may be thinking, "Whoa, I can't do that!" Do you believe you are unable to connect directly and personally with a source of spiritual guidance that can teach you, moment by moment, about loving yourself? Let me reassure you that anyone can learn to do this. I teach people how to do it every day. At first, they always think they are making up the information they receive, but with practice they receive such a profound experience of guidance that they realize it is available for every one of us.

What is your spiritual guidance like? It is whatever feels right for you: God, Goddess, Spirit, Higher Power, the Creator, Jesus, Allah, the Buddha, a saint, nature, energy, light, the All, Universal Intelligence, a guardian angel, a teacher or mentor, an Ascended Master, a deceased loved one (a person or an animal), a being or animal you invent, or simply the highest, wisest part of yourself: your own higher self. Regardless of what you imagine as your guidance, you will access the same profound love, comfort, and wisdom that is always here for all of us.

You can experience your spiritual guidance as within you, outside of you, or both. It can be something you visualize, something you feel emotionally, or both. It is whatever works for you to tap into the infinite wisdom that is available to us in the universe.

Practicing the six steps of Inner Bonding long enough gives you such a deep personal experience of being spiritually guided that you no longer have to take it on faith that loving guidance is here for you: you will know it through your own direct experience.

Before going further, let me tell you what happened with Marilyn, whom you met in the introduction to this book.

Marilyn, thirty-seven, is an Internet consultant. She and Jeff, thirty-six, who works in the entertainment industry, had fallen passionately in love three months prior to consulting with me. Neither had ever felt so in love before. Yet here they were, only a few months into their relationship, and the bloom was off the rose. I started to work with both of them after Marilyn's first session, in which she confessed she was terrified of being in love.

Neither of them knew anything about creating a safe inner space, so they could not create a safe relationship space. Consequently, as independent as Marilyn had been before meeting Jeff, she suddenly put her well-being into his hands. Then, because she had made him responsible for her safety and sense of worth, she had to control him to make sure she was safe. Because Marilyn did not have a strong loving adult or a spiritual connection, she was terrified of getting hurt.

As a small child, Marilyn had been left alone a lot. Her parents had taken care of her physical needs but not her emotional needs. She had often felt lonely and terrified. Now these feelings were back in full force. The moment Jeff was inattentive, out of town, or in some other way unavailable, Marilyn became terrified. She responded to her terror by getting angry, sarcastic, and saying mean things to Jeff, or by pulling back from him. Her anger and withdrawal were ways of trying to control his love for her. (Her mother had behaved the same way with her father.) Marilyn did not have a loving inner adult who knew how to handle rejection or the fear of rejection.

Marilyn was also afraid of engulfment because both of her parents had been very controlling with her, and she had always felt she had to give herself up to be loved by them. As soon as she and Jeff got really close, these fears of engulfment surfaced, and Marilyn went into anger or withdrawal. She had no loving inner adult who knew how to set limits that would prevent her from losing her sense of self. This is what had brought her into my office. This is why she broke down in her first session saying, "I'm deeply in love—and I'm terrified."

Jeff was raised to be the emotional support for his mother. His parents had divorced when he was small, and his mother was an immature, needy woman. Jeff learned to be her caretaker, and he moved right into that role with Marilyn. He allowed her to treat him badly. His fears of rejection were so great that he was willing to lose himself rather than risk losing her. At the same time, he was terrified of losing himself too much, so when things got really bad, he would completely close down, shutting Marilyn out. This would activate her terror of rejection, she would get angry, and a vicious circle would begin. The more Jeff complied or withdrew to control Marilyn's behavior, the worse her controlling behavior became. The angrier she became, the more he gave himself up or withdrew. This controlling system created a very unsafe relationship space.

Because neither Jeff nor Marilyn had developed a strong loving adult, neither could create a safe inner space or sustain a safe relationship space. As a result, the passion that had been so powerful just a few months earlier was waning.

Fortunately, both Marilyn and Jeff were willing to learn to become strong enough within themselves to love. They started practicing Inner Bonding and began developing their loving inner adults. They worked hard, and within a few months, both of them began to feel a deep sense of safety within themselves and within the relationship. A relationship that seemed to be heading for disaster turned around completely: Marilyn and Jeff have joyfully set a wedding date.

Let's move on to see what each of them did to create a loving adult capable of beginning to heal their fears of rejection and engulfment.

Creating the Loving Adult

The loving adult is who we are when we are open to learning and connected with an inner or outer spiritual source of guidance—when we are tapped into a source of knowledge and wisdom beyond the limited perspective of our wounded self.

In order to operate as loving adults throughout the day, we need to be able to tap into our guidance at will. We can't meditate for an hour every time we are confronted with a fearful situation. We need to be able to learn what is loving to ourselves at the very moment we need it. We need to be able to connect with our source of guidance instantly.

How do we do this?

Imagine that your mind is a receiver, like a TV. If you want to see a particular show, you select the channel, and your TV tunes in to the right airwave. Even though we can't see these airwaves, they are there in the atmosphere. They vibrate at a higher frequency than we do. To see and hear what these airwaves carry, we need to turn on our TV.

Universal information is just like information carried on TV airwaves: it exists at a higher frequency than we can see or hear. But you can learn to raise your frequency high enough to see, hear, or feel this universal information. The key to connecting to your spiritual guidance is learning how to raise your frequency.

Your frequency is the rate at which your energy vibrates. Our physical bodies vibrate at a low frequency so that we can see each other. Spirit vibrates at a high frequency, like the wings of a hummingbird, which is why most of us cannot see beings in spirit form. We can, however, learn to raise our energetic frequency high enough to feel and hear these spiritual beings, and some gifted people can see them.

One major key to raising your frequency, to turning on the TV set of your mind, is your intent. An intent to control lowers your frequency automatically, while an intent to learn about loving yourself and others automatically raises it.

When your deepest desire is to learn with Spirit about loving yourself and others, your frequency may become high enough to receive the information you need. Since you are in charge of your intent, in each and every moment you can learn to choose to learn with Spirit about loving yourself and others.

The other major key to raising and keeping your frequency high is about what you put into your body. The vibrancy of foods depends on how they are grown or raised.

Processed foods, with many chemicals in them, sugar and foods that turn into sugar in the body, vegetable oils such as safflower, sunflower, canola, soy, corn, and cottonseed oil, factory-farmed foods, GMO foods, foods with pesticides, foods grown on devitalized soil with chemical fertilizers all lower the frequency of your energy, making it harder to connect with your guidance. These foods, along with many drugs, destroy the gut flora, causing toxicity in the body and brain, making it hard to connect with your guidance. For more about keeping your frequency high enough to experience at-will divine connection read my recent books *Diet for Divine Connection: Beyond Junk Foods and Junk Thoughts to At-Will Spiritual Connection* and *The Inner Bonding Workbook: Six Steps to Healing Yourself and Connecting with Your Divine Guidance.*

Connecting with Your Spiritual Guidance

If you are not already connected with a personal source of spiritual guidance, you might be able to create it for yourself right now. In order to do this, you need to be willing to move into your imagination. I have a beautiful little sign on an end table that says, "Imagination is evidence of the Divine," by William Blake. Our imagination is a great gift from Spirit to help us connect with our guidance. When you allow yourself to imagine, you are opening the door to universal wisdom. This is a creative process—the same process that painters, musicians, writers, and other creative artists use to access original ideas. Ideas are like bits of energy that are always all around us, and creative people learn to use their imagination to access these ideas. You can learn to do the same thing to access information about what is in your highest good at any moment.

Imagine that you have found an old bottle. You rub it, and out comes a genie who says to you, "I will bring you your personal source of spiritual guidance, but you have to tell me the form in which you want this guidance to appear, because your guidance wants you to feel safe in its presence." Your guidance is the most loving, compassionate, powerful, and wise being or energy that you can imagine. It can come to you as a being, as a presence, or as light or energy. Go inside yourself now and feel what form would be most comfortable for you.

Creating an image for your spiritual guidance is a tool to help you to access the wisdom that is here for you. In reality, your guidance would probably appear as light, but sometimes an image is easier to relate to.

If you want your guidance to appear to you in human form, do you want a man or woman, or one of each? What age would you like this being to be? Do you want a mother or grandmother image? A father or grandfather image? Do you want someone your own age? Do you want the person to be of your race or a different race? It can be someone you have known, someone you make up, or someone you have seen in a dream. Or it can be the highest, wisest, and most loving aspect of yourself. If you want it to be an animal (such as Aslan in C.S. Lewis's Chronicles of Narnia series), it can be a pet or an imaginary animal, and it can communicate with you telepathically. It can be a religious figure that feels loving and safe to you. Perhaps you are more comfortable with just a light or a sense of presence, or your experience or concept of God. Imagine whatever form feels safe, loving, reliable, wise, and powerful to you. If being held or touched is important to you, create an image that you can cuddle up to and be held by—not a sexual image, but a caring and compassionate one, one that will comfort your inner child. If you want, you can give your guidance a name.

Now close your eyes and allow yourself to go inside and create an image of your spiritual guidance. Just use your imagination. There is no "right" way to do this. Let yourself move out of your mind and into your feelings. Let the feeling part of you—your inner child—choose whatever safe, loving, and powerful image feels best to you.

Whatever form you choose will work just fine, because it is the act of imagining and asking about your highest good with a deep desire to learn about what is loving to yourself that opens the door to universal information. The form that your spiritual guidance takes doesn't actually matter. It is your intent to learn, using your imagination, and feeding yourself clean food that opens you to the powerful information your guidance has for you.

The truth about your false beliefs and the information about loving action toward yourself can come to you in many different forms. Once you ask about the truth and about what is most loving in a particular situation, the answer may come immediately, or it may take some time. It may come in words that come through your mind, or as an image that pops into your mind. It may come as a feeling that motivates you to take a certain action. It may come through the words of a friend. The answer may leap off the page of a book you are reading. You may find it as you are surfing the Internet. It may come to you in a dream. You might fall asleep with a question on your mind and awake with the answer. When your deepest desire is to take full responsibility for your own emotions and behavior, and to learn about what is loving to you, your spiritual guidance will find a way to communicate with you.

Have you created your guide, your personal source of spiritual guidance? If you haven't, please take the time to do this now, as it is an essential aspect of the practice of Inner Bonding.

The image you have just created may change over time. That's fine as long as you feel safe and comfortable with it, and you feel that its presence is powerful and wise enough to help you become strong enough to love.

Now let's look at exactly what Marilyn and Jeff did to heal their fears and create a safe relationship space in which their love could thrive.

3

Six Steps to Inner Safety

I am going to bring you through all six steps at once in the hopes that you will begin to experience the power of these steps to create a strong, loving inner adult who can heal the fears and limiting beliefs of your wounded self and release your core soul self—your inner child—to express all that you are. In reality, each of these steps takes considerable practice. It is best to read this chapter when you have the time to go through the entire process.

To help you learn these steps, I will invent a conflict situation. As you imagine that you are facing this situation, I will walk you through the six steps to help you discover the loving action you can take. Let's say that you have put yourself under a lot of pressure at work to perform perfectly, and you are not getting your project done on time. You are hard on yourself when you don't perform up to your own expectations, and you tend to become self-critical. In addition, you have told your partner (we'll call this person Kris, so they can be either a man or a woman, depending on your circumstances) that you would be home by 7:00 p.m., but you realize late in the day that you need to work later. You know from past experience that when you call and say you are going to be late, Kris becomes upset and judgmental, and sometimes angry. You find yourself putting off making the phone call.

Step One: Willingness

Step One of Inner Bonding is the willingness to feel your emotions and take full responsibility for the thoughts and actions that cause the wounded feelings, and for lovingly managing and nurturing the core existential feelings of life.

To do this, bring to mind the situation we set up with your partner and really feel as if you are in that situation: you need to work late, and you have to call Kris to say so.

Now put your focus inside your body. Breathe into your chest, your solar plexus, your belly, your arms and legs, your head. Notice any physical sensations in your body, any tightness, tension, or fluttering.

Let's say that when you tune into your body, you discover tightness in the pit of your stomach, and you realize that you are feeling anxious. Your first thought is that this is because you are afraid you will be judged and yelled at by Kris. But let's explore a little further.

Imagine that the anxious part of you is a child—whatever age comes to mind is fine. Imagine that you open your arms to this anxious part of you, welcoming your anxious feelings. Don't try to make the feelings go away. Just move toward them rather than away from them, embracing them and gently holding the part of you that has these feelings.

What do you usually do when you feel anxious? If you are at work, do you work harder, procrastinate, pace back and forth, run out for a smoke, drink coffee, or yell at someone? If you are at home, do you turn on the TV, graze in the refrigerator, grab a beer or a cigarette, or take it out on your partner or your children by getting irritable, critical, or angry? Do you shut down, zone out, go into a fantasy? Do you call someone and keep them on the phone or try to get your partner's attention or approval? Do you act out sexually in some way? As we have seen, our wounded parts have a multitude of ways to avoid feeling our painful emotions.

Now, instead of doing any of your usual behaviors to control your feelings and get rid of them, open to them. Be with them, breathing into them and accepting them with compassion. Remind yourself that you have good reasons for your feelings, and that they are your inner guidance.

Step Two: Intent to Learn

Step Two of Inner Bonding is the conscious decision to move into the intent to learn about how you might be causing your painful wounded emotions and what might be happening externally that may be causing core painful feelings.

Begin by imagining the spiritual guidance you have just created for yourself. Surround the anxious part of yourself with that loving and compassionate energy, and invite it to come into your heart. Find the place in you that knows you have good reasons for feeling anxious: your limiting beliefs, which create your fears. Become curious about what you are thinking or doing that is causing this anxiety.

Now, in this moment, you are a loving adult, in the intent to learn.

Step Three: Inner Dialoguing

Step Three is dialoguing out loud or in writing with your feelings to discover the thoughts that are causing your anxiety, and dialoguing with your wounded self to learn about the false beliefs causing these thoughts. Step Three is also about dialoguing with the core feelings to understand what they are telling you about a person or situation. At other times when you are not distressed, you can also explore the needs, desires, and intrinsic worth of your core self.

This is where it is vital to be a loving adult. The loving adult is the only part of you that can dialogue with your feelings and explore the thoughts, beliefs, and situations that are causing your feelings. You cannot explore from your wounded self.

Again, imagine that your feelings are a child within: your inner child. Children give you truthful answers only when they feel safe enough to tell the truth. Since you are a loving adult only when you are open to learning and actively connected with your spiritual guidance, you must be sure to stay open to learning and staying connected with love as you move through Step Three.

There is a big difference between how a wounded part of you will explore your feelings and how you as a loving adult will explore them. A judgmental part of you might say to an anxious part, in a demanding, irritated, or judgmental tone, "Why are you so anxious?" The part of you that is anxious will not feel safe enough to respond truthfully. So another wounded part, one that believes you are a victim and that others cause all your feelings, will step in and say, "Of course I'm anxious! I don't like being judged and yelled at by Kris. What do you expect me to feel?"

But when your loving adult approaches the inner child with gentleness and caring, the dialogue might go like this:

Loving adult: You must have good reasons for feeling so anxious. What am I telling you or doing or not doing that is causing you to feel anxious?

Inner child: You don't take care of me when Kris judges me. You let him/her walk all over me and treat me badly. I feel alone and abandoned by you.

Loving adult: You're right. I do abandon you. Of course you feel anxious when I don't take care of you.

Inner child: Yes. Just like I felt when Mom didn't take care of me and didn't take care of herself with Dad [or vice versa]. I was always scared then, and now I'm scared with Kris.

Loving adult: What else do I do that is similar to when you were little?

Inner child: You tell me it's my fault when Kris is upset, that I didn't do something right. You make me do what Kris wants instead of what I want. I feel awful when you do that. And you always put a lot of pressure on me at work to do things perfectly. Then, if I don't get the work finished, you criticize me and make me feel worthless, just like Dad (or Mom) did. I always feel like I have to do everything right. You tell me I'm not OK unless other people like me and approve of me, so I have to say and do everything right. I hate this! I always feel so unsafe when you put this pressure on me and you don't show up for me.

It is easy to think that we are victims—that all our difficult feelings are caused by how others treat us rather than by how we treat ourselves or how we respond to others. But as you practice Inner Bonding, you will discover that your painful wounded feelings are caused by your own judgmental thoughts and your own self-abandoning behavior.

Many of us treat ourselves the way we were treated as children by our parents or other caregivers. In addition, we've learned to treat ourselves the way our parents treated themselves, since they were our role models. Unfortunately, most of our parents were not role models for loving self-care.

Now that you have listened to your inner child, you can go further into Step Three: exploring the false beliefs of the wounded self. Tune into the wounded, self-abandoning, self-critical part of you that pressures you to perform and doesn't take care of you when people are being unkind. This is a child or an adolescent part that learned to define your self-worth through others' approval and now wants control over getting that approval. Imagine your child or adolescent wounded part, and embrace him or her with compassion. This part of you is doing the best it can to take care of you and make you feel safe in the absence of a loving adult, having had little role modeling about how to be one.

Loving adult: I'd like to understand the good reasons you have for being so harsh and self-critical.

Wounded self: I have to get you to do things right. If you slack off or mess up, others will criticize me. They'll think I'm stupid or bad.

Your wounded self believes it can control you with self-criticism into doing things "right," and thereby control others into being accepting, approving, or nonjudgmental of you. Don't forget: the intent of the wounded self is always to control, so all self-critical behavior, as well as trying to do things right (or not taking care of ourselves and just giving in), is coming from an intent to control. Controlling is the only way the wounded self knows to try to feel safe.

Loving adult: There must a good reason why you believe it is best to give in to Kris.

Wounded self: Maybe Kris will get even more angry and leave if I don't give in. That really scares me.

Your wounded self is trying to control Kris by giving in. Because you have been abandoning yourself, your wounded self is terrified of being left by Kris and would rather give in than risk losing your partner.

Loving adult: You know, it doesn't seem to be working well to be self-critical. All it does is create anxiety, and people seem to criticize us anyway. Giving in and letting Kris yell at us isn't working well either. We just end up feeling awful. I know you are afraid of losing Kris, but I am learning to be here for you, and our spiritual guidance is here too.

You are not alone. I'd like to see if we can find a better way to handle things.

Step Four: Dialoguing with Your Guidance

Once you understand the thoughts and limiting beliefs within your wounded self that are underlying your anxiety, you can move to Step Four: learning with your spiritual guidance. Again, it is best to dialogue out loud or in writing. Your mind might wander if you do it silently, moving out of a loving adult state into your wounded self without realizing it.

Start Step Four by bringing to mind the spiritual guidance that you have already created. Take as much time as you need to get a firm image in your mind. Then find the place within you that deeply desires to know the truth about your limiting beliefs and to learn what the loving action toward yourself would be in this situation.

Now ask your spiritual guidance, "What is the truth about my belief that I can criticize myself into doing things right? What is the truth about my beliefs that doing things right or giving in will give me control over how others see me and feel about me?"

Since this is a dialogue, now imagine how your guidance might reply. Go ahead and make up the conversation between the two of you. When you have done the six steps of Inner Bonding often enough, you will have had many experiences of profound answers coming through to you, and you will know that there really is something guiding you, even though it may feel as if you are making it up. Whether you feel the answers are coming from within you, from without, or both is irrelevant. They will come when you ask questions with a sincere desire to learn.

The answers may not come immediately, so be patient. You may receive answers when you least expect them, like when you are in the shower or taking a walk. Just keep asking, and the answer will eventually come—in words, images, feelings, or dreams. When your intent is to learn, your guidance will find a way to communicate with you. It may say to you, as mine said to me when I was dealing with these issues:

You want to believe that you can control yourself with self-criticism. But self-criticism creates insecurity and anxiety. It makes it harder, not easier, to be fully yourself and fully confident in what you know. The anxiety and insecurity cut you off from the knowledge and creativity of your essential self.

You also want to believe that you can control how others feel about you and treat you by being nice and giving in. But look at it the other way around. Can others control how you feel about them? Can they control how you treat them? No. You decide for yourself how you feel about and treat others, and they decide this for themselves too. Also, no one likes to feel manipulated, and when others feel you trying to control them by acting perfect, being overly nice, or giving in, they may pull back from you. They may end up disrespecting you as well.

All the energy you are putting into trying to control others is exhausting you, and it's doing you no good at all. You don't have to be perfect and do everything right to be worthy and lovable. You don't have to give yourself up to be loved. Look inside at your core self. You have goodness, kindness, caring, compassion, and intelligence within you. Start to notice your own inner worth and lovability. Then you will not feel you have to always give in or work so hard to impress others. What others think won't matter so much anymore.

Your guidance may not say all this at once. But eventually you will receive enough information to understand which of your beliefs are false and limiting and what the truth is.

Next, ask your guidance what loving action you need to take toward yourself: "What do I need to be telling myself and doing differently so that I don't feel anxious about calling Kris and saying I'll be home late?"

Your guidance may say to you:

First of all, tell your wounded self that you are not bad if you work late, that you don't have to be perfect, and that you will not beat yourself up if you don't get home on time. Instead of either working too hard or giving in to Kris, look inside and see what you really want to do. Does it feel most caring to yourself to stay late or to leave work and go home? Make it OK not to be perfect. Tell yourself you can make mistakes without putting your entire worth on the line. Let mistakes be just a learning process, not a definition of your unworthiness.

Next, decide that you are going to be courageous enough to feel the loneliness and heartache, the crushed, shattered feeling you feel when Kris is angry and judgmental, and to take care of yourself if Kris is unloving. Acknowledge the loneliness and heartache with deep compassion toward yourself, and be willing to say to Kris, "It hurts my heart when you are angry and judgmental. We can discuss this, but only if you stop being harsh. Maybe we can also talk about why it is so upsetting to you when I'm late." You can tell your truth about not liking Kris's response to you and move into an intent to learn together. If Kris doesn't open up, however, you will need to end the conversation—to lovingly disengage.

This means that you have to decide beforehand that you are willing to lose Kris rather than continue to lose yourself. If you have made this decision, then you can end the conversation if Kris continues to be unloving. Letting your anxious part know that you are willing to disengage from the conversation rather than be treated badly will go a long way toward relieving your anxiety. Your anxiety comes more from the fear of allowing yourself to be treated badly than from actually being treated badly. Your anxiety will eventually go away if you consistently take the loving action of moving into compassion for your core existential pain and disengaging rather than reacting from your wounded self every time you are being treated badly. You must also help your inner child to keep from taking Kris's behavior personally. Kris's angry and judgmental behavior reflects what is going on within him or her. It is not about you.

The complete information about your beliefs and the loving action in a particular situation may come over time. Your guidance may steer you toward people who can help you discover the truth and suggest what loving action to take if you are not yet able to access this information yourself. Eventually, with enough practice, you will be able to access your guidance yourself.

Some time ago I asked my guidance, "How do I take care of myself when someone is blaming me, or angry at me, or dumping on me? What can I do when people's energy is negative? Do I need to say something to them, stand up for myself, let them know they can't treat me this way?"

"How do you feel when someone is being unloving?" she asked me.

"My heart hurts. Sometimes I feel lonely, and sometimes I have this heartache, and sometimes my heart feels broken, and I feel such sadness."

"Yes, this is what the heart feels when someone is being unloving. These are the core existential feelings of life, along with grief, helplessness over others, outrage over injustice, and fear of real and present danger. The first thing you need to do is put your hand on your heart and compassionately acknowledge the painful feeling. Invite me into your heart to help you to be caring, gentle, tender, kind, and understanding of these feelings. Then open to learning with me to learn about what these feelings are telling you and what the loving action is. These feelings are letting you know that the other person is in their wounded self, being unloving to you. If you ask me in the moment, I will let you know if it is your highest good to move into an intent to learn with the other person, or to lovingly disengage."

In order to lovingly disengage, you have to have reached the point in your life where you completely accept your lack of control over others' feelings and behavior. As long as you want to say something to try to get another person to stop what they are doing—such as defending, debating, or explaining—you are not ready to lovingly disengage.

There is a big difference between disengaging and withdrawing. When you disengage, you keep your heart open. Disengaging is a loving way of taking care of yourself. By contrast, when you withdraw, you close your heart. Withdrawal is a form of control—an attempt to punish the other person by withdrawing your love.

Most people become reactive in the face of conflict. They react with their own negativity from their wounded self, remain quiet, or withdraw. If they remain quiet or withdraw, they may react inwardly, ruminating about what the other person did:

"I just hate it when she dumps on me like that. Why does she have to be such a complainer?"

"He has no right to yell at me like that. Who does he think he is anyway?"

"I wish I had spoken up for myself when he criticized me. I wish I wasn't such a wimp."

"I am going to let her know how much she hurt my feelings."

These kinds of ruminations keep you stuck in the negativity of the interaction, even if you never say anything. These reactive thoughts pull you down, lowering your frequency and making you feel like a victim.

How can you disengage without withdrawing in anger or hurt? How can you take loving care of yourself rather than trying to control the other person? How can you avoid escalating the interaction with your own negative reactivity—your anger, blame, criticism, defensiveness, explanations, lectures, compliance, resistance, arguing, convincing, fighting, debating?

By compassionately acknowledging the heart hurt and staying completely present for the core pain until it moves through you, you can keep your heart open. You need to be willing to take your eyes completely off the other person and turn them inside, taking gentle, tender care of your own painful core feelings.

Once the pain has moved through, you can open to learning with your guidance about any other loving action you may need to take, such as taking a walk or calling a friend. If the other person has been physically or emotionally abusive, then it is very important to discover the loving action regarding getting out of the relationship, because staying in an abusive situation is never loving to yourself.

If you have been very compassionate with yourself, you will likely not have any residue from the interaction. You will have kept your heart open so that the next time you are around this person (provided it was without physical or emotional violence), you are able to be completely present and loving. You don't have to wait for an apology or get the other person to see what they did. Your loving behavior towards them is not determined by them, but by having taken loving care of yourself.

This is very magical not only for you, but for the relationship, because you are no longer reactive—no longer continuing the negative interaction with your own negativity. The other person's behavior tends to change, because when their anger, whining, blaming, or complaining elicits no response, even an energetic one, there is no longer any point in their behavior: you are not taking it personally and therefore do not feel punished by it.

When you completely let go of control and just take compassionate care of yourself, not only do you end up feeling great and empowered, but the good feelings between you and the other person often return very quickly.

Step Five: Taking the Loving Action

Step Five of Inner Bonding is taking the loving action that your guidance has told you to take.

In the scenario we have been using, this means telling yourself that you don't have to be perfect and do everything right. It means staying late if that's what is in your highest good, or leaving early if that is in your highest good. It means disengaging and compassionately attending to your heart hurt if Kris continues to be disrespectful toward you. It means making sure that your inner child does not take Kris's judgmental behavior personally.

You need to let your inner child know that your survival is not at stake as it was when you were very small and needed your parents to survive. In order to be willing to lose Kris rather than continue to lose yourself, you need to know you will be OK if you are alone. It may take some time practicing Inner Bonding before you feel strong enough to actually take these loving actions and risk losing Kris. But once you feel strong enough to love yourself, you can be in your truth and integrity with Kris regardless of the outcome.

Without taking loving action and creating inner safety, you will never heal your fears of rejection and engulfment, nor will you heal the limiting beliefs that cause these fears.

Becoming strong enough to love means having the courage to take loving action on your own behalf regardless of the outcome. When you are willing to do this, your inner child begins to feel loved, worthy, and safe. Through loving action toward yourself, you take back the power to define your own worth and thus create your own inner sense of safety.

Step Six: Evaluate

In Step Six, you evaluate your actions. How do you feel as a result? Are you feeling stronger, safer, less anxious, more peaceful and joyful? Are you feeling more valued and worthwhile because you have taken loving care of yourself?

If you are truly being loving to yourself—gently, kindly, compassionately embracing your core painful feelings and going to your guidance for other loving actions—you will find that your addictions gradually diminish. When you are no longer avoiding the core pain, you no longer need the protections against them.

However, some addictions are challenging even when you are taking care of yourself, because you may be both physically and emotionally addicted. When this is the case, good feelings may not be there immediately.

For example, a loving action such as stopping smoking will not result in immediate good feelings, so you will need to evaluate your long-term feelings. Often what feels good in the moment, such as getting angry, being compliant, eating, drinking, using drugs, smoking, spending, and so on, feels awful in the long run. Likewise, what feels scary in the short run, like lovingly disengaging or stopping a substance addiction, often feels really wonderful in the long run.

When evaluating the loving action you've taken, don't just notice your short-term feelings. Look to the long term. Eventually, if you continue to take loving action on your own behalf, you will begin to feel very safe and valued inside.

Back to Cal and Ruby
Let's get back to Cal and Ruby, the couple who broke up because Cal looked at other women and Ruby

became enraged. To sort this out, we first need to look at the bottom line: intent. From the beginning, Cal's intent was to have control over getting love and safety from a woman, while Ruby's intent was to have control over getting a man in order to define her worth and lovability. With the intent to control instead of to learn, their relationship was doomed from the start.

Neither Cal nor Ruby was intent on learning about their own feelings or taking responsibility for them. Neither was available to their own deeply painful feelings, having learned to protect against them in childhood. Neither had done their inner work to embrace and nurture their painful feelings and learn from them, so each was highly reactive to the other's controlling behavior.

Let's pretend that these same two people meet, but each is open to learning and taking responsibility for their own feelings. How are things different?

The first time Ruby sees Cal look at another woman, her insecurity is triggered. Because she has an intent to learn, she notices this and has a deep desire to understand what thoughts and beliefs within her are creating these feelings (Steps One and Two). Through practicing Inner Bonding, Ruby recognizes and embraces the fearful, jealous part of herself and explores her belief that her worth is based only on her looks (Steps Three and Four). She takes loving action for herself by sharing this with Cal, telling him about her childhood and her insecurity (Step Five). She tells him that she knows he has good reasons for looking at other women, and she tells him this not to have control over getting him to stop, but out of caring and curiosity.

Cal, instead of going into denial (a control tactic) about his addiction to looking at women, is curious to learn about his own unconscious behavior and about Ruby's feelings.

Through this process, which Cal and Ruby practice each time a conflict comes up, their understanding of themselves and each other grows (Step Six). Their intimacy deepens. Healing occurs as they come into truth instead of operating out of the false beliefs of the past. Ruby slowly learns to see herself through the eyes of her spiritual guidance, as well as through Cal's eyes. She sees that Cal is not her father and that his love for her is not based only on her looks. Cal tells Ruby what he values about her: her intuitiveness, understanding, compassion, creativity, and all the special little things that are just her. As Ruby sees herself through Cal's eyes and through the eyes of her guidance, she begins to define her worth internally.

As Cal explores his addiction to getting his safety through women, he sees clearly that as much as Ruby loves him, he feels safe only when he is there for himself as a loving adult. Cal sees that it is unrealistic for him to expect Ruby to always be there in the way he wants: she will still be angry or distant at times, since she is human. He also acknowledges that his inner safety cannot depend upon her being ideally loving.

Cal embraces the very young child within who wants and needs that ideal love and safety, and he learns to give it to himself.

Both Cal and Ruby learn to compassionately embrace their loneliness and heartache when the other becomes angry, judgmental, or distant, and learns to take loving action for themselves in the face of the other's controlling behavior. As a result of taking responsibility for their own feelings, their fears of rejection and engulfment gradually heal.

Now Cal and Ruby's love deepens daily instead of eroding, and all because of one thing: they are both devoted to becoming loving human beings with themselves and each other rather than controlling the other person's love. They are both devoted to creating a safe relationship space, using it to heal their woundedness, and becoming more loving to themselves and each other. They embrace the journey of evolving their own souls. Instead of giving themselves up or attempting to get their partner to give themselves up, they support each other in becoming all they can be.

What if you are reading this and you are excited about learning, but your partner, whom you love, has no interest in opening to learning? Can you have a loving relationship without your partner doing his or her inner work?

The answer is yes! When you learn to take loving care of yourself, taking responsibility for your feelings and creating a safe inner space, you can continue to share your love with your partner. You might not have the depth of intimacy that is possible with two open people. You might need to learn to deal with conflict by lovingly disengaging and making your own decisions about a particular situation, since there may be no safe arena for resolving conflict. But if you care deeply for your partner and you don't want to leave the relationship, creating a safe inner space will bring you so much joy that you may be able to let go of having a safe relationship space.

The more you learn to take full responsibility for your own feelings of pain and joy, the more likely your partner will eventually open. After all, the main reason people don't want to open to learning in conflict is that they are afraid of being attacked and judged. The more you learn to take loving care of yourself, the less you will have your eyes on your partner. When you learn to approach your partner with curiosity rather than an intent to control, you are doing your part in creating a safe relationship space. Once your partner feels safe from criticism, he or she might open to learning.

Using the Six Steps to Define Your Worth

Inner Bonding can be used not only to explore inner conflicts and conflicts with others but also to define your own worth.

Let's try it now. Sit down in a comfortable place with a photo of yourself as a small child. Let yourself become absorbed in this picture.

Tune in to how you feel about this child. Do you see him or her as lovable or as a burden? Is this child worth your energy and attention? Do you value the way this child feels?

Now imagine that this child—which represents the feeling part of you and is your inner guidance system—is within you right now. Notice how you are feeling in this moment. Are you peaceful, happy, relaxed, excited to be alive? Or are you tense, anxious, fearful, sad, hurt, angry, depressed? Do you feel full or empty inside? Noticing your feelings with the intent to take full responsibility for them is Step One of Inner Bonding.

Now move into Step Two. Breathe into your heart and consciously choose to learn about your current feelings. Imagine your spiritual guidance, inviting the love and compassion of your guidance into your heart by simply saying, "I invite you into my heart."

Move into Step Three. Dialogue with the feeling part of you, your inner child, to learn about what you are doing that may be causing your feelings. If you are feeling happy and peaceful, notice what you are thinking, doing, or saying to yourself that is creating these positive feelings. If you are feeling anxious, hurt, angry, guilty, shamed, or depressed, notice what you are thinking, doing, or saying to yourself that is causing these feelings. If you are feeling sorrow, loneliness, heartbreak, or grief, bring loving comfort to yourself. Sometimes holding a stuffed animal or a doll can help bring comfort to your hurting heart.

For the sake of an example, let's suppose you have noticed that you are feeling anxious about a presentation you have to give at work (Step One) and have moved into an intent to learn about what is causing your anxiety (Step Two). Dialogue with your inner child to find out what you are thinking about giving this presentation (Step Three). Are you telling yourself that if others don't like it, you will be a failure? Perhaps you think that your worth as a person is connected with how well you do the presentation. (Making your worth dependent on your performance will always cause performance anxiety).

Now ask your spiritual guidance, "If my worth is not in my performance, what is my worth?" Imagine that your guidance is speaking to the little child in the photo you are holding (Step Four). Your guidance may say something like, "Your worth is based on your sweet nature, your love of play, your smile, which lights up the room. You are an inherently good person, and your goodness is not dependent upon your performance. You have courage. You are curious. You are creative. You are lovable no matter how your presentation is received." Your guidance will help you to see who you are inside, in your beautiful soul—the immortal part of you.

Seeing the truth of who you really are is only half of what needs to happen for you to feel worthy within. Once you see the truth, you also need to know what loving actions you need to take based on this truth (also Step Four). If you see the beauty of your soul but continue to treat yourself badly by drinking heavily, eating badly, giving yourself up to others, ignoring your feelings, judging yourself, and so on, you will never feel inherently worthy and lovable. You need to both see the truth and take actions based on it in order to feel a deep inner sense of worth.

Ask your guidance, "If I am truly worthy and lovable, what do I need to do for my inner child for him or her to know this?" In the case of giving a presentation at work, your guidance may say, "Let your inner child know that you will continue to love him (or her) even if you make mistakes." If you are exploring general self-worth issues, your guidance might say things like, "You need to pay more attention to your emotions." "You need to notice how critical of yourself you are and learn to be more accepting." "You need to sit and hold your stuffed animal [or doll] for fifteen minutes every day while bringing in love to yourself." "You need more rest and playtime." "You need to eat better." "You need to stop smoking (or drinking)." "You need to clean up your living space." "You need to compassionately be with your loneliness and heartbreak." "You need to speak your truth to your partner." "You need to stop taking responsibility for your partner's feelings." If you are truly open, you will receive a message from your guidance about how to take better care of yourself.

Step Five calls for you to follow through by taking the loving action that your guidance recommended. Without this step, the first four steps mean nothing.

After you have taken the loving action, you need to check in again with how you are feeling and evaluate the effectiveness of the action. Evaluating is Step Six of Inner Bonding.

If you do this process daily whenever you are feeling anything less than peaceful inside, you will slowly redefine yourself while learning to take responsibility for your feelings.

You have just been through two brief Inner Bonding processes to begin to create inner safety and become strong enough to love. This is just the beginning! Once you learn to create a safe inner space and define your own worth instead of depending upon others to define it, you can easily learn to create safe relationship spaces.

A Quick Reference Guide to the Six Steps

Inner Bonding works only when you practice it frequently throughout the day. Below is a summary of the Six Steps to help guide you through the process.

STEP ONE: WILLINGNESS

Choose to notice your feelings and be willing to feel both your wounded pain and your core pain. Be willing to take responsibility for the thoughts and actions that are causing your wounded pain, and lovingly embrace your core pain. Also, be willing to take responsibility for creating your own peace and joy and for defining your own worth.

STEP TWO: THE INTENT TO LEARN

Choose the intent to learn to love yourself and others instead of the intent to control and avoid. Choosing to learn opens your heart to your spiritual guidance and moves you into your loving adult.

STEP THREE: DIALOGUE WITH YOUR INNER CHILD AND YOUR WOUNDED SELF

Choose to welcome, embrace, and learn from your emotions. Discover your thoughts, beliefs, and the behaviors that result from them, coming from your wounded self, that are causing your painful wounded feelings. Explore what your core feelings are telling you about a person or a situation. Explore, too, your gifts and what brings joy to your core self.

STEP FOUR: DIALOGUE WITH YOUR GUIDANCE

Dialogue with your spiritual guidance, opening to learning about the truth about any beliefs you've discovered. Explore the truth about who you really are. Discover the loving action toward yourself that your guidance recommends.

STEP FIVE: TAKE THE LOVING ACTION

Take the loving action you discovered Step Four, putting love into action.

STEP SIX: EVALUATE

Evaluate the effectiveness of your loving action.

4

Unsafe Relationship Systems

It is often easy to see how another person is creating an unsafe relationship space, but it may be difficult to see your own controlling behavior. If you are in a relationship that is having problems, it's important to understand that both of you are creating the unsafe relationship system. The only thing you can do to change it is to become aware of and shift your own contribution to the unsafe system by changing your intent from controlling and avoiding to learning about loving.

Unsafe relationship systems result from combinations of various forms of overt and covert control. One partner might be controlling overtly, with anger, blame, and demands, and the other might be controlling covertly, with compliance, withdrawal, or resistance.

This chapter includes many examples of couples or families creating unsafe relationship spaces.

Do you identity with any of these? If you do, be sure not to judge yourself. There is much for you to learn through these examples, but only if you don't judge yourself, because self-judgment stops learning.

Simone and Bradley

Simone consulted with me because she had been dating Bradley for two years and was trying to decide whether to marry him or move on. She is a successful thirty-six-year-old dentist who wants very much to have children, and she felt that her biological clock was running out of time. She loved Bradley but often did not feel loved by him. I asked her to have a joint Skype session with him (I work with people on the phone, Zoom, and Skype) because I needed to experience the energy between them in order to understand their relationship system.

Bradley, forty and a successful physician, said he loved Simone and wanted very much to marry her. Yet he was constantly withdrawing in anger the moment there was any conflict, and he would remain withdrawn for weeks at a time. At the moment he withdrew, he would send Simone darts of anger and blame, saying extremely hurtful things to her. His intent was clearly to control rather than to learn. Simone, having learned early in her life to avoid her feelings of loneliness and heartbreak, would respond by getting defensive or giving herself up, not only to avoid her own core painful feelings, but to get Bradley's approval and avoid his disapproval.

As we explored their relationship system, it became apparent that Bradley had an extreme fear of engulfment, while Simone had a deep fear of rejection and abandonment, having lost both of her parents at a young age. The moment Simone tried to control Bradley by pulling on him in any way—for attention, approval, or enthusiasm—Bradley's deep fear of engulfment would surface. Instead of embracing his core painful feelings—the loneliness and heartache that started with his mother's controlling behavior—and wanting to learn about his fear, Bradley would protect against being controlled by saying something mean to distance Simone; then, just to make sure he didn't lose himself in any way, he would withdraw to feel safe. This would further trigger Simone's hurt and abandonment fears. Instead of wanting to learn about them, she would get angry, blaming, and defensive in order to stop Bradley from being mean and withdrawing. Simone and Bradley were constantly dumping their negative energy on each other in their attempts at control. Their reactions to their fears and their core pain eroded the safe relationship space.

I pointed out that each of them was contributing equally to creating an unsafe relationship system, and that if each of them committed to working on themselves and developing their own loving adult, they could learn to create a safe relationship space.

Simone was deeply desirous of doing this work, but Bradley wasn't interested. He was too afraid of his core pain, so he convinced himself that the problem was completely Simone's: if she just stopped blaming and pulling on him, everything would be fine.

Simone worked on creating her own inner safety and was able to let go of her pulling and blaming behavior. However, nothing changed in the system. If anything, the more loving Simone was, the more negative and mean Bradley became. His deep fears of losing himself in an intimate relationship were triggered even more by intimacy than by Simone's controlling behavior. In reality, it was not her behavior that was causing Bradley's fears: they were there way before he met her. For Bradley, a loving person ignited his fears even more than a controlling one, because he knew he was more likely to give himself up to someone he really loved. He felt safe only as long as he could be distant from Simone, while blaming her for it.

It didn't take long for Simone to recognize that if she wanted a loving relationship, she needed to move on. The more she learned about taking good care of herself and creating a safe inner space, the less she was willing to be at the other end of Bradley's (or anyone's) mean and negative energy. Simone left Bradley, not in anger and blame, but in a state of personal power, ready to create a safe relationship space with an open, caring man.

Sometimes when one person shifts their part of an unhealthy system, it moves toward healing, but, as here, this obviously is not always the case. Simone had to be willing to lose Bradley rather than continuing to lose herself in this unsafe relationship system.

Doing inner work to become strong enough to love enabled her to let go of a relationship that was never going to work for her. Because we attract at our common level of woundedness or health, Simone was eventually able to attract a man with whom she could create a safe and loving relationship.

Tony and Ari

Tony, twenty-nine, owns a beauty salon, and Ari, thirty-six, is an architect. They have been together only six months and already find themselves endlessly bickering. The following incident happened a few days before they had a session with me. They were at Tony's mother's house with his brother and his brother's two sons, ages five and seven. Tony was reading on the couch, and Ari was playing with the boys, who were kicking and hitting each other. Ari told them to stop: "Hey, guys, cut it out! Stop trying to hurt each other!"

Tony heard a harsh tone in Ari's voice that he didn't like and reprimanded him in front of the boys by saying in a critical tone, "I'm uncomfortable with how you are talking to the boys."

Tony thought he was just sharing his feelings with Ari, but he was actually blaming Ari and making him responsible for his own uncomfortable feelings. His primary motive was to control rather than to learn. This violated the safe relationship space between them.

Ari was mortified at being scolded in front of the boys and asked Tony to come into the other room. He proceeded to explain to Tony why he had said what he did to the boys, hoping that his explanation would control how Tony felt about him. In doing this, Ari was now violating their safe relationship space with a covert form of control: *explaining*.

Explaining is not always an attempt to control: it depends upon the intent. Sometimes explaining is just giving information or sharing your point of view, especially if someone has asked for the information, but in this case Ari's intent was to control how Tony felt about him by explaining his point of view. Ari had no intent to learn about why he did what he did and why Tony felt upset about it.

Tony felt manipulated by Ari's explanation, and they ended up in a fight, each believing that the other was at fault, which further eroded the safety of their relationship space.

During the fight, they each said things that further eroded this safety. Tony insisted that the problem was Ari's tone of voice with the boys. "It's your issue, not mine," he yelled. Ari countered with a threat to the relationship: "I can't handle being treated like this anymore. I just want out." Shaken by this, Tony shifted his intent, asking Ari with true curiosity if he really meant it. Ari then stomped out, saying, "I don't want to talk about it."

Both Tony and Ari indulged in numerous controlling behaviors that eroded the safe relationship space:

- Blaming each other.
- Anger and scolding.
- Explaining themselves in an effort to control the other's point of view.
- Making it all one person's fault: "It's your problem, not mine."
- Having one foot out the door, verbally threatening the relationship.
- Withdrawing and refusing to talk about the conflict. It is appropriate to disengage when one or both partners are closed, but being unavailable when the other partner opens to learning is controlling and will erode the safe relationship space.

As a result of their unloving behavior, Tony and Ari both ended up feeling angry, righteous, anxious, and unsafe.

If Tony had intended to safeguard the space between them, he would first have been compassionate with his own discomfort, acknowledging that he felt some heartache in the face of Ari's harshness. Then he would have asked Ari to come into the other room before saying anything about Ari's behavior with the boys. Then Tony would have told Ari that his harsh tone with the boys was painful to him and would have opened to learning about the good reasons Ari had for using that tone.

Ari would have preserved the space by being open to learning with Tony about why he, Ari, used that harsh, controlling tone of voice. Or, if Tony had already violated the space with his scolding, Ari could have asked him to go into the other room. Instead of explaining, Ari could have let Tony know that his tone felt violating and hurtful. He could have opened to learning about what Tony was feeling and what fears were behind his critical, controlling tone.

Both of them could have taken responsibility for their controlling, critical behavior and learned about the fears and beliefs behind it. By taking responsibility for their own feelings and behavior, being open to learning about themselves and the other, and caring about how their behavior affected their relationship space, they would have created intimacy rather than distance.

If either Tony or Ari had been open to learning about the other or taking loving care of themselves, the entire interaction would have gone differently. They would not have escalated the conflict. Later, when things had calmed down, they might have been able to explore and learn from the conflict.

Axel, Patricia, and Jonathan

Axel, forty-eight, a plumber, is married to Patricia, forty-five, a bookkeeper. They are the parents of Jonathan, age fourteen. They decided to consult with me because they didn't know what to do about Jonathan, who was drinking a lot. On the way over to their second session, the three of them had a conflict in the car about Jonathan coming home late the night before. Jonathan came into my office visibly upset with his parents. During the session, he tried to tell his father why.

"It's your tone. I hate it."

"I just need you to let us know when you will be home and follow through on what you say," Axel replied.

"I know, Dad. I'm not talking about that. I'm talking about your tone."

"I don't know what tone you are talking about," Axel retorted, with a menacing edge in his voice. Then he began to yell. "I'm just worried about you. We are your parents, and we have a right to know when you will be home."

Axel and Jonathan were struggling with a typical relationship difficulty: Jonathan was referring to Axel's intent to control rather than the issue of lateness, while Axel was trying to talk about the issue itself. Jonathan was focused on intent, while Axel focused on content. There is no way to resolve a conflict when two people are focused on such different aspects of it. The issue itself—Jonathan being late and not calling—cannot be explored and resolved until both people are open to learning.

"How do you feel when your father speaks to you like that?" I asked Jonathan.

Tears welled up, and his voice was choked. "I feel awful. But what's the point of talking about it? He never listens to what I have to say." It was obvious that his father's anger was deeply painful to Jonathan.

Axel's voice became even more like a razor blade as he continued to berate Jonathan. I could feel him dumping his controlling, negative energy on all of us. I looked at Patricia to see how she was dealing with this. She looked glazed over, completely absent, shutting out her own hurt.

"What are you feeling, Patricia?" I asked gently.

"Nothing," she replied as tears welled up in her eyes. She looked scared. She didn't know what to do. She had no idea how to deal with her own core pain, take loving care of her inner child, or be there for Jonathan.

As the session progressed, it became apparent that while his parents were certainly not responsible for Jonathan's choice to drink, it was the only way he had found to feel safe in his house. He had started drinking when he was eleven after finding some of his parents' alcohol. For a couple of years, he just drank at home; now it was extending to the rest of his life. But he didn't know any other way of handling his feelings. Jonathan was doing what he had learned to do from his parents: trying to control his feelings instead of taking responsibility for them.

I could clearly see that Jonathan was a sensitive boy and that Axel's razor-sharp tone cut him to the quick, creating an extremely unsafe relationship space between them. I could also see that Axel was in complete denial of his abusive tone of voice, which indicated his intent to control. He believed it was OK to dump his negative, angry, judgmental energy all over the people around him. This was creating unsafe relationship spaces with both his son and his wife, and neither knew how to handle it in a loving way toward themselves.

Since Axel was not open to learning, I ended up working in future sessions with Jonathan and Patricia, helping them learn to take care of themselves when they were treated badly. Since Patricia didn't want to leave Axel, the best way I could support them was to help them learn to take loving care of themselves when Axel was triggered into his verbally abusive wounded self. Both Jonathan and Patricia learned to be compassionate with their loneliness and heartbreak, and to disengage when Axel was verbally abusive. Both learned to stop taking Axel's behavior personally or trying to control him with their arguing or compliance. As Jonathan learned to take loving action for himself in the face of his father's violating energy, and his mother learned to emotionally support herself and him, Jonathan gradually stopped drinking. He had learned how to create a safe inner space, even though he could not create a safe relationship space with his father.

Many people violate a relationship space by dumping negative energy on others. Most of us would not think of throwing darts at people, yet we often throw energy darts. When you feel a tightening in your stomach or solar plexus and a heaviness in your heart, you might have received an energy dart from someone's unloving behavior, from someone's anger, blame, judgment, fear, anxiety, or self-pity—that is, from someone's intent to control. Many people don't think about how their energy affects others. Yet in order to create a safe relationship space, we need to take responsibility for the energy we put out. Dumping our negative energy on others will always result in an unsafe relationship space.

Shelby and Murray

Shelby and Murray are in their early forties and work together in Murray's family retail business. When they came to see me, they had been married for nine years and had been locked into a frustrating, unsafe relationship system for most of that time. Murray's major complaint was that he couldn't trust Shelby because she wasn't honest. She would tell him she would do something that he asked her to do, like call the electrician, and then she wouldn't do it. Murray would then feel frustrated and angry, and would blow up at her. This happened over and over. Murray was thinking of getting a divorce.

When we looked deeper into their system, it became apparent that when Murray asked Shelby to do something, the energy behind his question was that of a demand, not a request. In addition, Murray usually handed Shelby the responsibility for his feelings, demanding that she give him the attention, acknowledgment, and compassion that he was not giving himself. Then he blamed her when she didn't support him enough.

As a child, Shelby had learned to protect herself from the heartbreak caused by her controlling mother by overtly complying while covertly resisting. She was now doing the same thing with Murray. When he demanded something of her, she would say yes even if she didn't want to, hoping to get him off her back, and knowing that if she said no, he would be furious. Then her resistance would take over, and she would fade away from the conversation or completely forget to do the task. Then she would be upset with herself, unable to understand why she kept fogging out and forgetting things. Not only was Murray judging her, she was judging herself, believing that the problems between them were all her fault.

Shelby and Murray did eventually realize that they were both creating the unsafe relationship system: Murray, by trying to control with his demands, anger, and judgment, and Shelby, by trying to control through resisting and not speaking her truth. But neither was devoted to consistently doing their Inner Bonding work. Neither was willing to learn to compassionately take responsibility for the core painful feelings that came up when the other was unloving. Rather than embrace his loneliness, heartache, heartbreak, and helplessness over Shelby, Murray stayed stuck in being a victim of her resistance; rather than learning to speak up in the face of Murray's demands, Shelby continued to shut down and resist.

These two did stay together, but they never reclaimed the passion and intimacy that was there at the beginning of their relationship, because they didn't have the courage to take responsibility for their existential pain. Instead, they continued to avoid it with their controlling behavior. They preferred the illusion of safety that it gave them rather than doing the inner work to create a safe relationship space.

Katrina and Nicole

Katrina, age twenty-two, moved back in with her mom and dad while attending graduate school in economics. After having lived alone, she found living with her mother difficult. Nicole had always been a highly critical person, but she had been especially hard on Katrina, her eldest daughter. It seemed to Katrina that she could never do anything right in her mother's eyes. Geographical distance had made their relationship easier to handle, but now that she was home, Katrina found her mother's criticisms intolerable.

Nicole commented on everything in a critical tone: what Katrina was wearing, what she was eating, how she spent her time, and so on. Katrina handled this by staying away from her mother as much as possible, not eating at home and going to her room as soon as she came in.

Now Nicole was angry at Katrina for not spending any time with her. "Why don't you eat dinner with us? Why don't you talk to me and tell me what is going on in your life?" she would ask in a hard, critical tone. It was more of a demand than a real question. Nicole didn't really want to know why Katrina wasn't spending time with her: she just wanted control over her.

Katrina would make up excuses, and the situation persisted. Katrina had about reached her limit. Moving out would create a financial problem, but she could do it. Still, she really wanted a connection with her mother. She knew that healing their relationship was important for her own growth, but she didn't know how to begin.

Both Nicole and Katrina had contributed to creating an unsafe relationship system. Nicole fed the system with her criticism, while Katrina contributed by withdrawing and withholding her truth while silently resenting and blaming her mother. When Katrina first consulted with me, it was easy for her to see her mother's end of the system, but it was very difficult for her to see her own.

There were many reasons why Katrina was not speaking her truth: she was afraid her mother wouldn't care about her truth; she was afraid it would bring more criticism; she was afraid her mother would kick her out; she was afraid it would mean the end of their relationship and there would be no chance to heal.

Katrina worked with me on learning to open to her authentic core feelings, which she was hiding with her withdrawal. She became aware of how heartbroken she has always felt when her mother criticized her. She learned to be in deep compassion for herself whenever her mother criticized her, embracing her hurting inner child with caring, kindness, gentleness, tenderness, and understanding. She learned to lovingly disengage, keeping her heart open, rather than closing her heart and withdrawing.

Finally Katrina reached the point where she was willing to lose her relationship with her mother rather than continue to lose herself. She was ready to tell the truth to her mother, not in order to change her, but to take care of herself and open to learning.

Even telling the truth can be a manipulation if its intent is to get the other to change. It is only when telling your truth is about taking responsibility for yourself (part of Step Five of Inner Bonding: taking loving action) that it is not a manipulation. Then it has no agenda for the other person. Telling the truth enables you to keep your heart open and stay open to learning with yourself and the other person.

The next time Nicole criticized her, instead of defending or explaining herself or withdrawing in anger, Katrina spoke her truth, gently, from her loving adult: "Mom, when you criticize me, it really hurts me." Then she opened to learning: "There must be a good reason you are so critical. I'd like to understand it."

"You know it's just the way I am. I am just a critical person," responded Nicole.

"Are you saying you believe you were born critical?" asked Katrina.

"No, but I've been this way most of my life."

"Was your mother critical of you?"

"Yes, of course!"

"How did you feel about it?"

"Oh, I don't know. It's just how she was."

"But how did you feel as you were growing up? Did you feel loved, or did you feel lonely?"

At this point, Nicole got quiet. Her eyes filled with tears. "Lonely. I felt so lonely. I still do. I feel lonely with your father. I feel lonely with you. You are never around. You never talk to me. You don't tell me what is going on in your life."

"I feel lonely when I'm with you too, Mom. I feel lonely when you criticize me, just like you felt with your mother."

Nicole started to sob, and Katrina held her. Together they cried for their own loneliness and for each other's. The connection that Katrina had always yearned for with her mother was beginning, because she had the courage to take care of herself by speaking her truth and moving into an intent to learn. Katrina and Nicole had begun to create a safe relationship space.

If Nicole had not opened up with Katrina, their connection would not have occurred, nor would the safe space have developed. Yet even if Nicole had not opened, Katrina would still have felt better for having taken care of herself by speaking her truth and having an intent to learn. She would no longer feel like a victim, even if her mother never opened. She would feel sorrow and grief over having to accept a lack of connection with her mother, but she would still have had a deep connection with herself and her spiritual guidance. She would feel safe within herself, even without a safe relationship space with her mother.

It is always harder to take the risk of taking care of yourself, telling your truth, and opening to learning when you have something to lose. Taking this risk is particularly difficult with partners, children, parents, and close friends. It is also difficult with employers, who may fire you, or employees, who may quit without giving you notice. It takes ongoing inner work to reach the place within where we are willing to lose the other rather than lose ourselves. But when a person comes to this place, they find that whatever the outcome, they are happier, healthier, and more fulfilled than if they had kept giving themselves up. If they get fired, a more fulfilling job appears. If they lose a relationship, they either find that they are happier alone or they find a more loving one. Whatever the outcome, they are far happier than they were as victims of and participants in an unloving, unsafe relationship system.

At my intensives, the couples, both heterosexual and same-sex, are always amazed at the similarities among their systems. These are easier to see when couples watch other couples work than when they are dealing with their own systems.

The most common system is some variation of this: Franchesca and Hanley have been married for sixteen years. Franchesca's major complaint is that

Hanley is often angry or resistant and withdrawn. In either case, he is not emotionally available to her. She feels resentful and lonely, and pulls on Hanley with her anger, criticism, blame, and complaints. Franchesca blames Hanley for her unhappiness, believing that if he changed, she would be happy. Additionally, she feels pulled on sexually. If she gives in to his demands for sex, she feels used, and if she doesn't, she feels emotionally rejected.

Hanley's major complaint is that Franchesca is often unhappy and upset no matter how much he does for her, and she is rarely sexually responsive. He feels burdened by her pull on him to make her happy, angry at her criticism of him, and deprived of a good sexual relationship. He is lonely and unfulfilled in the marriage and blames his feelings on Franchesca's bitchiness and sexual unresponsiveness. He feels victimized by her behavior. He believes that if she would change, he would be happy.

In variations on this system, one partner (usually the wife) is upset about, feels shut out by, or feels burdened by the other's drinking, watching TV, overworking, underworking, and so on. One or the other partner may be angry at carrying most or all of the financial burden, especially if the other tends to spend too much money.

Sometimes this scenario is reversed: the man feels shut out emotionally and the woman feels rejected sexually. Sometimes one partner feels shut out both emotionally and sexually, while the other feels angry and withdrawn at feeling pulled at and controlled.

Often one partner is the caretaker and feels overwhelmed by the other's resistance to taking responsibility around the house or to granting requests that the partner makes.

Often the wife is the caretaker and the husband is resistant to her requests to take out the garbage, spend time together, or explore conflict. She feels resentful and rejected, while he feels resentful and controlled. Again, this scenario can be reversed, with the man as the caretaker and the woman as the resister. Perhaps he earns all the money, then comes home and takes care of everything, including the children, while she spends her time playing tennis, spending money, taking classes, and resisting responsibility for the house and children.

While unsafe relationship systems differ in their details, they all have one thing in common: neither partner is taking responsibility for their own feelings and needs. Both are abandoning themselves and, in one way or another, making the other person responsible for their happiness, safety, and sense of lovability and worth. Both are controlling, though in different ways. Neither is open to their core painful feelings of loneliness, heartache, heartbreak, sorrow, grief, and helplessness over each other, and neither has learned to lovingly manage these feelings. In all of these systems, controlling is more important to the partners than learning about loving.

Taking and Caretaking:
The Codependent Relationship System

There is a huge difference between creating a safe relationship space and taking responsibility for another's internal sense of safety. The latter is called *caretaking*. We are caring when we give to others with no strings attached. We are caretaking when we give to others with an agenda attached, such as getting approval or sex. We are care giving when we are doing for others what they cannot do for themselves, such as taking care of children, the elderly, or the ill. We are caretaking when we attempt to do for others what only they can do for themselves, such as taking responsibility for their feelings of inner safety, lovability, and worth.

When we make others responsible for our feelings, inner safety, and sense of worth, we are being takers. Takers hand over their inner child to the other person, getting angry and blaming when the other person doesn't do what they want. Caretakers also make the other person responsible for their feelings, but in a more covert way. Caretakers ignore their own feelings while taking responsibility for another's feelings, hoping that the other will then take care of the caretaker's feelings. When the taker just keeps on taking without caring about the caretaker, the latter may eventually get angry or ill.

Most caretakers believe that their "selflessness" is truly loving, and takers readily support this belief. In fact, our society usually defines love in this way. But looking deeper, we can see that both taking and care-taking are controlling behaviors, addictions that allow a person to avoid responsibility for their feelings.

Laura and Jack

Laura is an accountant, tall and slender with fiery red hair, and Jack is an artist and a heavy drinker. Laura was the epitome of the caretaker, constantly giving herself up as her way to control Jack. She had sex whenever Jack wanted even when she had no desire for him. She took care of everything in the house, including their two young sons, and worked full-time as the primary wage earner. She never told Jack how she felt because she was afraid to hurt his feelings. She believed that taking care of herself was selfish, that being a good person meant giving herself up to take care of others.

Laura attended an Inner Bonding workshop but was afraid to pursue Inner Bonding for herself because she feared that Jack would not join her and her growth would mean the end of their marriage. She stayed in her unhappiness, feeling deeply lonely, for two more years before deciding to attend an Inner Bonding Intensive. There she became fully aware of her role in the relationship system, acting as the care-taker for others while avoiding all responsibility for herself. With support from the group, Laura gained the courage to open to learning about loving herself, and she began to diligently practice Inner Bonding.

As Laura had predicted, Jack was furious with the change in her. He called her selfish. He drank more. He cried and became pathetic, hoping to make her feel guilty. Then he stopped drinking and started being "nice," helping more with the kids and around the house. He even appeared to join her in the intent to learn by attending an Inner Bonding workshop and joining her in some sessions with me. But he was doing all this only to manipulate Laura into giving him what he wanted. The moment she did not behave as he wanted, Jack became furious again. He was not intent on becoming a loving person with himself and others; he was motivated only by the desire to get love.

Sometimes Laura was confused because Jack was acting so differently, yet in her gut things still felt the same. She still felt pressured to give Jack love, and she still felt no love in return. She still felt lonely around him. Laura stayed steadfast, trusting her feelings rather than his new behavior or the words he was saying.

It didn't take long for Jack to give up his manipulation and go back to drinking and being angry much of the time. The changes he had made were not coming from his own deep desire to learn to be a loving person. Instead, he was using Inner Bonding as another way to control. Anything can be used as a means of control; it just depends on the intent.

Jack's "loving" actions had an outcome attached: to get Laura to take care of him again and have sex with him whenever he wanted it. When this didn't work, he decided there was no point in making nice and went back to his old ways. Even though he had professed his deep love for Laura, she discovered that he was already seeking a girlfriend to take care of his "needs." It was crystal clear to Laura that Jack had no intention of learning to take responsibility for his own feelings, so she decided to get a divorce.

What she had been afraid to face in the past now became her freedom. She reached out to friends to whom Jack had previously objected, and she no longer felt lonely. Her fear of being alone, which had kept her in a lonely, unhappy relationship, vanished as she experience the joy of taking care of herself and her children without being burdened by Jack's angry, demanding behavior.

Larry and Heather

Let's look at another unsafe relationship system that revolves around taking and caretaking. Larry, forty-one, is an elementary school teacher, and Heather, thirty-five, is a massage therapist. They have been married for five years. They consulted with me because they seemed to be in endless conflict. Heather is often very judgmental of herself. She generally ignores her own feelings, blames Larry for them, and demands that he do this, that, or the other so she'll feel better. No matter how caring Larry is with her (and he is often accepting and compassionate), Heather does not feel an inner sense of safety, because she is treating herself badly.

Neither Larry nor Heather experiences being in a safe relationship space. For Larry, the reason seems obvious: Heather's blaming anger violates the safety of the space. But Heather doesn't feel safe either, because the moment she makes Larry responsible for her inner sense of safety, she becomes a victim of his choices. As long as Heather's inner safety depends on Larry doing what she wants him to do, she will feel victimized when he doesn't. She cannot feel safe in the relationship space without a safe inner space. When Heather's well-being and sense of worth are determined by Larry's behavior, there is no safe inner space for her. Choosing to define herself externally leaves her feeling vulnerable and unsafe. Her fears of rejection and engulfment, which are based on her refusal to take responsibility for her feelings and define her own worth, preclude any sense of safety.

Larry participates in creating their unsafe relationship space whenever he becomes Heather's caretaker. When Larry is caretaking, he is ignoring his own feelings and needs. He is putting his inner child in a closet and trying to take care of Heather's inner child so she will feel safe enough to open to him. He does everything he can to create a safe space for her, but nothing to create a safe space for himself. By choosing to be a caretaker, Larry is attempting to control Heather's behavior and feelings. He hopes that by taking responsibility for Heather's inner child (instead of his own), she will feel loved enough and will heal enough to take care of his inner child.

In other words, he is giving up himself in order to be loved by her.

Meanwhile, Larry's inner child continues to feel unsafe, both inside and in the relationship. Larry continues to tolerate Heather's angry, blaming behavior even though her behavior is creating a very unsafe relationship space for him. This is because Larry is addicted to caretaking. Whenever he feels anxious about being rejected by Heather, he tries to control this feeling by caretaking her. Yet until he stops taking responsibility for Heather's inner sense of safety and starts taking responsibility for his own, it is unlikely that she will give up her angry, pulling, blaming behavior. Heather is equally addicted to getting Larry to take responsibility for her feelings, and is unlikely to break this addiction as long as it seemingly works for her.

Like Larry's addiction to caretaking, an addiction gets its teeth into us because it pacifies our anxiety over feeling our core painful feelings. All addictive behavior results from a desire to avoid feelings that we are afraid to feel because we think that they will overwhelm us. Addictions are the pacifiers and anesthetics the wounded self turns to when our core painful feelings and fears of rejection and engulfment are activated, and there is no inner loving adult to step in. If our loving adult were there to handle our feelings of loneliness, heartbreak, and helplessness when others are rejecting or engulfing, we would not need our addictions.

Whenever Larry takes responsibility for Heather's anxiety by attempting to pacify her wounded self, they both feel better for the moment. But Larry's caretaking perpetuates the unsafe relationship system. Only when he stops enabling Heather to avoid her painful feelings will she be forced to handle them herself. At that point, she may decide to take responsibility for her inner safety, or she may look for another addiction to try to feel safe—another person, sex, a drug, and so on. Larry has no control over which choice Heather makes. As long as he is more afraid of losing her than of losing himself, he will continue to participate in his addiction of caretaking, and the relationship space will remain unsafe.

In addition, Larry may continue to caretake as long as he receives momentary relief from his own fears in the form of some connection with Heather. Until either Larry or Heather is unhappy enough to break the cycle, they will continue to live in an unsafe relationship system.

When having a loving relationship becomes more important to them than trying to control each other, Larry and Heather will do the inner work necessary to take responsibility for their own feelings and become strong enough to love. Once they consistently show up as loving adults for themselves and individually create safe inner spaces, they will be able to be loving adults with each other, thus creating a safe relationship space.

Until I started to practice Inner Bonding, I never realized that I did not have a safe inner space, nor did I expect others to create their own inner safety. Instead, I jumped in to try to create a safe relationship space with others. I believed that if only I were loving enough, the other person would open and be loving back. Then I would feel safe, loved, and not lonely. I tried so hard, yet I always felt lonely anyway. Often, when others persisted in staying closed, I would become angry and judgmental, self-righteously blaming them for the problems between us, never realizing that my caretaking was a form of control. Inside I believed that I could control the safety of our relationship space by being caring and accepting, all the while ignoring my own feelings and needs. Because I believed that, I never considered that we each had equal responsibility in creating a safe relationship space.

The Devotion to the Illusion of External Safety

Because we have free will, we can each choose what is most important to us in life. We choose whether it is more important to learn to be a loving human being so we can feel safe internally or to control others so we can try to feel safe externally.

Herbert is a good example of a person who has chosen control instead of love. A businessman in his late forties, Herbert is often very loving with others. He is charming, funny, intelligent, and very helpful when his wife or children come to him with their problems—until they trigger his fear. Then he sulks and retreats behind a wall of ice, staying there until someone in his family makes it safe enough for him to open his heart again. His wife or children have to apologize and take full responsibility for the problem before he will come out from behind his wall. His wife often spends exhausting hours pacifying Herbert's wounded self before he will open and share his love again. Herbert takes no responsibility for making himself feel safe enough to open his heart, or for creating a safe relationship space.

Renee, a successful actress about the same age as Herbert, is another example of a person who has chosen external safety over loving. Much like Herbert, Renee is incredibly charismatic when she is open. In her open state she is fun, loving, and affectionate. But the moment she feels criticized or her husband or children don't do exactly what she wants, she becomes a different person. Blaming and rageful, she screams at her family that they don't care about her. She stays in her angry funk until her husband or children comply or apologize and, again like Herbert, she takes no responsibility for her end of the relationship, or for her inner safety.

Daniel's outward behavior is not nearly as extreme as Herbert's or Renee's, yet his deepest devotion is also to having control. An attorney in his thirties, Daniel is small and a little round. He enters most situations with guardedness, erecting a hard barrier around his heart. There is a slight edge in

his voice and a feeling that you are being watched—
and you are. Daniel is watching to see if you are open
or closed before he decides whether he will be open
or closed. He does not want to take the risk of being
open and getting rejected, so he closes his heart until
he feels that his external environment is safe. In conversation, Daniel tends to use his charm, humor, and
verbal ability to get the attention he seeks. Getting
attention is his way of feeling validated. Daniel talks
on and on about himself, demanding others' attention as a way to define his worth. Like Herbert and
Renee, Daniel makes others responsible for his feelings of safety. His guarded approach to others makes
a safe relationship space impossible.

Daniel believes he is taking good care of himself
by keeping his heart closed until others make him
feel safe. He believes it is better to be prepared for
anger, blame, criticism, or judgment by keeping his
shield up. He also believes he is being interesting
instead of controlling when he talks a lot. He has not
learned to be a loving adult for his own inner child.
He has not learned to take care of himself in the
face of invasive behavior. He has not learned how to
keep from taking others' behavior personally so that
he can stay open in the face of rejection, nor has he
learned to define his own worth.

In choosing the path of external safety, Daniel has
made both his choice about whether to be open and
his ability to feel safe dependent upon the behavior of
others. Because he has not developed a loving adult

who has learned how to create inner safety regardless of others' behavior, he has put his wounded self in charge of making him feel safe and worthy (which it does by setting up a barricade and demanding attention).

Herbert, Renee, and Daniel are all deeply devoted to having control over their feelings of safety in the external world rather than learning to be loving to themselves internally and sharing their love with others. They are not yet on the path to becoming strong enough to love.

5

Creating Safe Relationship Spaces

A safe relationship space is present when two people choose as their highest priority to be loving with themselves and with each other. It is a sacred space where the spirit of love, rather than judgment and control, predominates. In a safe relationship space, the people involved are willing to take full responsibility for their own feelings, while accepting that their behavior affects their partner.

You create a safe relationship space when

1. Each person fully accepts that they are a part of an energy system in which their behavior deeply affects their partner, and is willing to take full responsibility for all their own feelings, energy, and behavior.

2. Each person is willing to compassionately feel their core painful feelings rather than avoiding them with protective, controlling behavior.

3. Each person is willing to take full responsibility for responding to the controlling energy and behavior of their partner from their own loving adult, open to their core painful feelings, rather than from their wounded self, trying to control the other person to protect against their core pain.

A safe relationship space is a circle of loving energy that results from each person's deep desire to learn about what is most loving to themselves and others.

To create a safe relationship space, the people involved need to be deeply committed to learning about their own wounded self—their controlling behavior and false beliefs—rather than focusing on their partner's controlling behavior. Each person needs to be learning to create a safe inner space that will make them strong enough to love. Rather than giving up themselves to avoid rejection (or trying to get their partner to give themselves up), both people are devoted to the highest good for themselves and their partner. Both are supporting themselves and their partner in becoming all they can be.

Any two or more people who want to learn to create a safe relationship space can do so. You can learn to create a safe relationship space, not just with a partner, but also with one or more friends, family members, coworkers, employees, and so on, provided everyone is willing to learn how to create their own safe inner space.

Safe relationship spaces are created when the people involved are devoted to the spiritual values of caring, understanding, compassion, collaboration, and honesty rather than to the earthly values of competition, power, and control over others.

Regina and Ken

Regina, thirty-two, is a stay-at-home mother with children from her previous marriage. She and Ken, thirty-nine, had been together less than a year when their old patterns, which had not been healed in previous relationships, emerged. Ken often came home from his job as the head of a large manufacturing company feeling anxious, depressed, and exhausted. He often complained to Regina about how sick he felt and how difficult things were at work, yet he did nothing to change that situation.

Regina felt annoyed when Ken complained and continued to avoid responsibility for his health and work issues. When she offered advice, he would get furious and resistant, telling her to back off and stop acting like a parent. Regina often felt frightened by Ken's anger and collapsed into angry tears, blaming Ken for her upset feelings. Ken then felt angry at being blamed and guilty that he had upset Regina, and he retreated by going to sleep early or going out drinking with his friends. Regina was left with her children and her misery, unable to sleep.

In this system, Ken was not taking responsibility for his health, his anxiety, his depression, and his work problems. Instead, he was being a victim. He used alcohol to avoid his feelings, or he complained to Regina, dumping his negative energy onto her and handing her responsibility for his wounded feelings. Ken pulled on Regina for sympathy rather than moving into compassion for himself and taking loving action on his own behalf. When he received advice or criticism from Regina instead of sympathy, he got enraged. He then blamed her for his rage instead of opening to learning about what was happening between them.

Regina was not taking responsibility for her feelings and needs either. She did not move into compassion for her own loneliness and heartbreak when Ken was angry, blaming, and complaining. Nor did she lovingly disengage when Ken dumped his anxiety and depression on her; instead, she gave herself up and listened to his complaints or became needy, angry, parental, and critical. Regina kept hoping that if she were angry enough, she could get Ken to take responsibility for himself; then she would not have to take care of herself in the face of his behavior. She felt victimized by his anger rather than moving into compassion for herself and taking loving action on her own behalf.

Both Regina and Ken were locked into the intent to control. The love and passion that had been so fulfilling at the beginning of their relationship was gone. Did they both pick the wrong person once again? Probably not. Regina and Ken could be perfect for each other—if they opened to learning about their respective sides of the unsafe relationship system they had created. Each was triggering the other's deepest fears of rejection and engulfment, and deepest core pain of loneliness, heartbreak, and helplessness.

But this painful situation had a silver lining. It gave them the opportunity to heal their deepest fears, if they chose to do so. When both partners open to learning, relationships that trigger our deepest fears can become the most powerful arena for healing those fears.

Regina and Ken did decide to hang in and deal with their problems. They came to an Inner Bonding Intensive together and began to face their fears of being rejected and controlled by each other. They learned to turn to the six steps of Inner Bonding and take care of their own feelings instead of blaming each other for them. They learned to tell their truth to each other without judgment or blame. Regina was finally able to say to Ken, "I feel so lonely when you drink, and I lose respect for you when I see you using alcohol to avoid your feelings. I know you have good reasons for drinking, and I would really like to understand what they are. What are you afraid of feeling?"

They also learned to take care of themselves around violating, invasive behavior. When Regina was angry or critical, Ken learned to say, "I feel so lonely when you blame and criticize me. If you are unhappy about something, let's talk about it, but I don't want to be treated badly." If Regina was not open, Ken learned to lovingly disengage, with kindness and compassion toward his core pain. When Ken complained, Regina learned to lovingly disengage with compassion for her loneliness and heartache, saying to Ken, "Honey, this doesn't feel good. I'm happy to help you if you want help, but if you are just going to complain, I'm going to go read."

Regina and Ken learned to help each other explore their controlling behavior instead of blaming it on each other. Through doing their inner work, they gradually became strong enough to love. Within a few months of dedicated Inner Bonding work, love and passion returned to their relationship.

The wonderful thing is that it is never too late to create a loving relationship system. No matter how awful things have been in the past, when two people decide to do their own inner work and create safe inner spaces for themselves, they can succeed in creating a safe relationship space.

Relationships as Energy Systems

In order to fully understand safe relationship spaces, we need to see relationships as systems where energy flows back and forth between the partners. In a relationship, each person's energy affects the whole. If one person changes, the whole system changes, which is why it is so important for you to be doing your inner work, even if the other person is not. Your own shift from the intent to protect, avoid, and control to the intent to learn about what is loving will deeply affect the energy of any relationship you are in.

Every relationship has a system. Some are healthy and safe, and others are not. These systems can start surprisingly early, sometimes within the first minutes or days of meeting each other. This was most apparent to me at one of my five-day intensives that I did at retreat centers before COVID, and that are now online. At these events, I work with twelve to thirteen people, working deeply with the Inner Bonding process for five full days. At this particular in-person intensive, two people, Janna and Aaron, met for the first time and had an instant "soul" connection. It was not a romantic connection; it was more like one between brother and sister. Both were married but saw an opportunity to do some deep healing with each other.

Janna, a clothing designer in her mid-thirties, was deeply wounded from having had an emotionally unavailable father. Janna had an intense and persistent fear that her husband, Lowell, would emotionally disconnect from her. As a result, she often reacted by becoming irritated or withdrawing from Lowell when he was even slightly detached because he was tired or preoccupied. Lowell would then react to Janna's reaction by becoming even more unavailable, which left Janna feeling hurt and confused. Janna and Lowell loved each other deeply, yet the relationship system they had created was preventing a consistent sharing of their love.

Aaron, a teacher in his late thirties, was deeply wounded from having had an emotionally incestuous mother, who used him to meet her emotional needs for a husband. She had made Aaron responsible for assuaging the loneliness she felt as a result of her lack of connection with Aaron's father, and had also allowed her sexual energy to spill over onto Aaron. As an adult, Aaron had such a deep fear of engulfment and being made responsible for his wife's feelings that he was often emotionally unavailable to her, even though he deeply desired connection. The more Aaron withdrew, the more his wife, Susan, wanted connection. They were in the same negative, unsafe system as Janna and Lowell.

When Aaron and Janna met at my intensive, their fears were not activated, so they connected deeply. They found themselves laughing, playing, and feeling safe with each other. They felt so safe the first day they met that they shared what was happening in their marriages.

This open sharing lasted about a day. The next day Janna wanted the same deep level of connection with Aaron that she had experienced the previous day, but her pulling energy of expectation triggered his fear of being responsible for someone else's feelings. He felt engulfed by Janna's expectations and reacted by putting up a wall. Within two days of meeting, Janna and Aaron had created the same system with each other that they had with their spouses.

Luckily, they had the safe space of the intensive in which to explore the system they had created. As they talked, Janna made the connection between her behavior with Aaron and her behavior with Lowell. She realized that she had only been aware of Lowell's disconnection from her, not of her own needy expectation of his continuing their deep connection or her compelling need for Lowell to take responsibility for her well-being. She saw that she had become addicted to connection with Lowell. Janna used her time in the intensive to learn how to stay connected with her core self and her spiritual guidance, and to compassionately feel her loneliness and heartache rather than pulling for connection with others. As part of her healing process, she talked to her husband on the phone during the intensive, and she was able to stay connected with herself in the face of his disconnected energy. She was thrilled to discover that when she did this, Lowell became far more present and connected with her!

Aaron also made important discoveries about himself. He realized that he had never thought about a loving way of responding to his wife's demand for connection. The only way he knew to handle his fear of engulfment was to put up a wall between them. Aaron learned that he could take responsibility for his own fears of engulfment by saying to Susan, "I'm feeling pulled on to take responsibility for your feelings and your well-being, and I don't want that responsibility. I get so scared of being smothered and gobbled up by you that I just want to run away. But I love you, and I don't really want to run away. Can we talk about what is happening between us right now?" He learned that if Susan wasn't open to learning at that moment, he could lovingly disengage, keeping his heart open rather than withdrawing behind a closed heart. By speaking his truth about himself, or by disengaging but compassionately keeping his heart open to his own feelings, Aaron found that he felt safe; he no longer needed to close his heart and withdraw.

Aaron also learned that speaking his truth was not about stating what he thought Susan was doing, feeling, or wanting. That would not be his truth; it would be his opinion. His truth concerned only his own feelings, experiences, and desires. By telling the truth about himself without blaming Susan or making her responsible for his feelings, Aaron could open the door to exploration and intimacy: maybe Susan really was pulling on him, or maybe Aaron was just afraid that she would do what his mother did. Only by speaking his truth with a deep desire to learn about himself and his wife would he be able to improve the safety of their relationship space.

Breaking the Pattern

In our current culture, if a relationship, or even a marriage, isn't working, we often just up and leave. A good reason not to act so quickly is that until we become strong enough to love, we will repeat the same patterns in future relationships. These patterns will inevitably emerge until we develop a loving adult self who can take care of our painful feelings and heal the wounded parts of us.

All of us, in various degrees, have fears of rejection and engulfment that are carried by our wounded selves. That's why it is a waste of time to leave a relationship (unless there is physical or emotional abuse) until we develop a loving adult who can stay open to learning or lovingly disengage in the face of fear. We cannot hope to stay open with another until we can stay open to our own core painful feelings. We cannot create a safe relationship space until we create a safe inner space. Having this safe inner space makes us strong enough to love.

Many people find that the same relationship issues show up over and over until they heal them—whether the relationship is with a relative, friend, coworker, or partner. Brenda, a retired teacher in her late fifties, spent much of her session time with me exploring her relationship with her sister, Fran. Fran would complain a lot to Brenda, but wouldn't address the cause of her complaints. She would come to Brenda as a victim, wanting Brenda's sympathy but not wanting her help. Fran had no intention of taking loving action on her own behalf. She was deeply invested in remaining a victim. Because Brenda believed that in order to be a good person, she needed to "fix" Fran, she would constantly offer suggestions about how Fran could help herself. Fran would then blow up at Brenda, accusing her of acting righteous and parental. Brenda would end up confused and hurt because she was "just trying to help." Eventually, Brenda backed off from her relationship with Fran without really understanding her own participation in the system.

Then Brenda met and fell in love with Loretta, a bank manager in her early sixties. For the first few months, Brenda and Loretta were passionately in love with each other. Then, inevitably, their controlling system manifested, and suddenly the passion was gone. As Brenda and I explored her relationship with Loretta, she was shocked to discover that it was just like her relationship with her sister Fran. Loretta would complain to her about problems at work or about her health, and when Brenda tried to offer suggestions (because that's what she needed to do for people to see her as a good person), Loretta withdrew. When Brenda persisted in offering advice to "fix" her, Loretta would shut down, eventually becoming angry and accusing Brenda of being invasive and controlling. Brenda, of course, was confused and hurt because she was "just trying to help."

As we explored her system with Loretta, Brenda realized that her wounded self felt validated when others did things her way. She was not just offering help, she was deeply invested in Fran and Loretta agreeing with her and doing what she suggested. Brenda saw that she believed that her worth, lovability, and goodness depended upon others taking her advice.

Brenda also discovered that when Fran and Loretta complained about their problems, she felt pulled on by them. She felt pressure to sympathize with their unhappy circumstances, which occurred because they were not taking responsibility for themselves. Brenda realized that when Fran or Loretta did not take loving care of themselves, she felt lonely around them, and her heart ached for their inner children. She realized that her "fixing" was a way of avoiding her own core painful feelings. She was trying to be the loving adult for Fran and Loretta's wounded inner children in order to take away her own loneliness and heartache.

Over time, Brenda learned to stop trying to get her sister and her partner to be loving adults to themselves and disengaged from the system. When the complaining started, she either told them she didn't want to hear complaints if they weren't willing to do anything about them or simply ended the conversation. These responses left her feeling much better. Eventually Loretta stopped complaining and started exploring her own addiction to being a victim. When Brenda and Loretta each took responsibility for their own end of the system, they were able to create a safe relationship space.

As for Fran, she did not open to exploring her end of the system, but with Brenda no longer participating in the old pattern, the dynamic between them changed. They never did create a safe relationship space, because Fran did not have the intent to learn, but with Brenda no longer listening to Fran's complaints and trying to fix them, Fran gradually stopped complaining. There was no point in complaining when no one was listening!

Because we take ourselves with us wherever we go, we will continue to create unhappy relationship systems with others until we are willing to take full responsibility for whatever we are feeling. The great gift that relationships can give us is the opportunity to become aware of the core existential feelings of life we are avoiding with our wounded selves and to see what needs healing. The great gift of a safe relationship space is an arena in which to do this profound healing work.

Shawn and Patti

Shawn, a screenwriter, and Patti, a set designer, are in their mid-thirties. Both professed to wanting to settle down and have a family. They met a year ago, and Patti had taken her time in getting to know Shawn, while Shawn had been impatient for a commitment. They had had an active and fulfilling sex life until Patti finally said that she loved Shawn and was ready for a more committed relationship. From that moment, Shawn had difficulty maintaining an erection. Patti was deeply distressed about this, sensing that something about her moving forward had created the problem. Rather than embracing her heartache, she reacted to it by getting angry at Shawn, wanting control over his withdrawal. Shawn, too, was distressed. He realized that this had been a pattern in his relationships in the past. He was interested as long as the woman was unattainable. But as soon as she was available, Shawn lost interest.

Shawn came in to see me alone because he was tired of this pattern and was ready to change it. He really did want to settle down and have a family, and he really did love Patti and didn't want to lose her, so he was perplexed by the situation.

As Shawn did his Inner Bonding work, it soon became apparent that, as much as he wanted a loving relationship, there was something his wounded self wanted even more: control over getting another's love. When a woman was unavailable, Shawn felt safe in attempting to have control over gaining her love. But the moment she gave him her love of her own free will, his fears of rejection and engulfment surfaced. If she gave him love of her own free will, she could also pull it back of her own free will, which triggered his fears. Shawn felt much safer when he was in pursuit of her love than when he actually acquired it. Once he had love, he feared losing it or losing himself in his attempt to keep it.

Shawn saw that having control over getting love was actually more important to him than giving and receiving it. He did not have a loving inner adult capable of creating a safe inner space. Because of this lack, he feared losing Patti's love (which was what defined his worth). He also feared that he would give himself up to Patti, allowing himself to be controlled by her in order to have control over her anger and her love. Shawn's fears of rejection and engulfment led to his feeling too unsafe to respond to her love. His lack of erection was the result of his fear.

As Shawn began to notice that his intent in his interactions with Patti was to control rather than to give and receive love, the door opened for him to make a new decision. He decided to face his fears of rejection and engulfment rather than protecting against them by trying to control. He started practicing the six steps of Inner Bonding throughout each day and established a strong connection with his spiritual guidance, which helped him manage his fears when they arose. Shawn was deeply gratified to find that as he began to feel safer within, the relationship space with Patti began to feel safer as well. He and Patti were able to explore their fears rather than protect against them with their various ways of controlling. As they learned to create a safe relationship space, Shawn's ability to respond sexually returned.

Shawn's problem is not unusual. I have discovered that many people believe they want love, passion, and commitment, only to find themselves withdrawing and turning off when they finally get what they thought they wanted. As much as they may want to share love and passion, what they want even more is control over getting the love and passion. This creates a very confusing situation for the partner. When the partner moves toward them, as Patti did, the other person moves back. Then, when the partner also moves back, the other person moves forward again. Because of this system, the couple will not be able to come together into a true sharing of love until they develop their loving inner adult selves through Inner Bonding and creating a safe inner space and a safe relationship space.

Getting Love versus Sharing Love

You might intuitively know that the highest experience in life is the sharing of love, but are you mistaking the idea of sharing love with the idea of getting love? The wounded self seeks to get love and avoid pain, which results in an inability to share love. We do not have love to share with others if we are empty of love within, and inner emptiness is one is the inevitable results of self-abandonment. Two empty people can never create a safe relationship space, because each will constantly pull on the other to fill their emptiness. Two people full of love have a deep need to share that love, and their fullness and sharing of love creates the safe relationship space.

On the earthly level, devoting oneself to getting love and approval from others is the norm, which creates unsafe relationship spaces. On the spiritual level, devoting oneself to learning how to truly care about oneself and others creates safe relationship spaces and advances the evolution of the soul's ability to love.

When we view a relationship as a system between two or more people instead of attempting to place the blame on one person, we create an arena for learning and healing. As each person learns to love themselves, they become filled with love, and their love overflows. By sharing this overflowing love with each other, their loneliness vanishes and is replaced by the deep joy of connection, creativity, and grace.

Virginia and Anton

Virginia, who owns a restaurant, and Anton, who has an import business, are in their fifties and have been married for about seven years. They love each other very much, yet they often found themselves feeling distant and unhappy around each other.

A typical situation occurred the day before they had a session with me. They had made love and were feeling very close. The next morning Anton got up much earlier than Virginia, as he usually did, and went into the other room to exercise. Two hours later, Virginia came into the room with open arms, wanting to recreate the connection they had the night before. But instead of allowing the connection to naturally occur, she was trying to make it happen with her pulling energy—trying to have control over getting love rather than giving and sharing her love. Anton felt the energetic pull from Virginia, which triggered his heartache and fear of engulfment, and he reacted to his pain and fear by retreating, trying to avoid being controlled by Virginia's pulling, needy energy.

Virginia, unwilling to feel her loneliness when Anton withdrew, went into her wounded self, feeling hurt and rejected. She saw herself as a victim of Anton's behavior and told him in a blaming tone that she felt hurt by his closed heart. Anton then blamed Virginia for his withdrawal, saying he was withdrawing because she was pulling on him for love and connection. Virginia denied pulling on him, saying she was just wanting to connect.

In this interaction, both partners violated the safe relationship space in their efforts to control and avoid being controlled. Virginia violated the space by trying to get love rather than give it and share it. Anton violated it by withdrawing. Virginia then violated the space again by making Anton responsible for her pain, while Anton violated it by blaming Virginia for his withdrawal. Then Virginia continued to violate the space by denying that she had been pulling on Anton for love in the first place. Neither was open to their core pain or to learning about themselves or each other.

Once again, let's see how things might have gone differently. If Anton had been compassionate toward himself regarding the heartache he feels when Virginia pulls on him, he could have spoken his truth from his loving adult rather than allowing his wounded self to withdraw. Then he could have opened to learning about the fears behind Virginia's controlling behavior. If Virginia had been willing to explore her pulling, needy behavior rather than denying it, they could have ended up feeling loving and connected instead of distant and angry. In addition, they might have discovered the root cause of the frequent distance in their relationship system.

In fact, when they did this exploration in their session with me, Virginia was able to see that her lack of trust stemmed from her father's emotional distance. Her wounded self was projecting her father onto her husband.

Also, Anton was able to see that his resistance to Virginia's pulling went back to his childhood—to feeling completely controlled by his mother. Whenever Virginia pulled on him for anything, he immediately felt like a three-year-old and became stubborn and resistant, as he had as a child. By each exploring their own part of the relationship system they had created, Virginia and Anton began to notice their choices in the moment. Once they were aware of their intent to control, they gradually became able to make new choices.

Selfishness versus Self-Responsibility

One of the last things any of us want to be called is "selfish." We often end up doing things we don't want to do to avoid being seen that way. In my counseling work with people, I often hear the questions, "Am I being selfish if I take care of myself instead of everyone else?" "Am I selfish if I do what I want instead of what someone else wants me to do?"

The problem occurs because of an inaccurate definition of *selfish*. We are being selfish when

- We expect others to give themselves up for us.
- We make others responsible for our feelings of pain and joy and blame them when they don't.
- We get angry at others for doing what they want to do rather than what we want them to do.
- We consistently make our own feelings, wants, needs, and desires important without considering those of others.
- We believe we are entitled to special treatment, such as being listened to even when the other person is tired or busy.

We are being *self-responsible* when

- We take care of our own feelings, wants, desires, and needs rather than expecting others to take care of us.
- We support others in doing what brings them joy, even when they are not doing what we want them to do.
- We show caring toward others for the joy it gives us rather than out of fear, obligation, or guilt.
- We have the courage to take loving action on our own behalf, even if someone becomes angry with us. For example, you go to bed early because you are tired, even if your partner gets angry at you for not watching a movie with him or her.

- We have the courage to speak our truth about what we will or will not do and what we do or do not feel, rather than giving ourselves up to avoid criticism, anger, or rejection.

Giving ourselves up to avoid being called selfish is not self-responsible: it is manipulative and dishonest. When we give ourselves up to avoid criticism, we are trying to control how another feels about us.

Taking loving care of ourselves, with no intent to harm another, is self-responsible. Yet we are often called "selfish" when we take care of ourselves. For example, Tammy had signed up to take one of my weekend workshops and was really looking forward to it. She let her husband, Frank, and two children know weeks before the workshop that she was going and that it was important to her. The day before the workshop Frank was given four great tickets to a basketball game. He wanted Tammy to go with him the next day, which was the first day of the workshop. When she said no, he got angry at her and told her she was selfish for doing what she wanted to do rather than spending the time with the family. Tammy came to the workshop with much to work on!

In reality, Frank was being selfish in expecting Tammy to give herself up rather than doing what was really important to her. He was not caring at all about Tammy; he just wanted what he wanted. He felt entitled to be angry at her when she didn't give in to his demands.

For Tammy, this was a crazy-making situation. Being labeled as selfish when it is really the other person who is being selfish is projection, and is crazy-making. Many of us grew up with parents who behaved in this way, demanding that we give ourselves up for them and telling us we were selfish when we were taking responsibility for our own happiness and well-being.

It is important for each of us to define selfishness and self-responsibility for ourselves so that we do not depend upon others' definitions. When you become secure in knowing that you not only have the right, but the responsibility, to support your own joy and highest good (with no intent to harm another), you will not be tempted to give yourself up when someone tells you that you are selfish for not doing what he or she wants you to do. When we are secure in knowing that our own intent is a loving one, we do not have to manipulate others into defining us as caring.

The Devotion to Internal Safety: The Basis of Creating a Safe Relationship Space

When your deepest devotion is to learning to be a loving human being, and you understand that the reason you are on this planet is to learn about and evolve your lovingness, joy, and the full manifestation of your inherent gifts and talents, your lovingness does not depend upon the intent or behavior of others.

Jodie, forty-six, is an interior designer. She has done much inner work to overcome her abusive family background, and she offers us a wonderful example of a person deeply devoted to loving. It's not that she is always able to maintain the intent to learn, or that she is always open and loving. She is not a fully enlightened being, able to stay open and loving no matter what. Her fears of rejection and engulfment still get triggered. The difference is that when Jodie's heart is closed behind her anger or withdrawal, she does not wait for anyone else to fix it. No one needs to apologize or pacify her. No one needs to "make nice" to coax her into being open and loving again.

Instead, Jodie goes within and does Inner Bonding, exploring her wounded self: the fears, thoughts, and limiting beliefs that triggered her fears, and the controlling responses that result. She works with her spiritual guidance to compassionately bring love to her core pain and truth to the wounded parts of herself. She also learns in what way she did not take care of herself in the situation that triggered her anger or withdrawal. Jodie learns which loving actions on behalf of her inner child would create safety within, then reenters the relationship, sharing her discoveries with her loved ones. If she needs help in this process, she seeks it from people competent to help her. She takes full responsibility for healing her emotional wounds and creating a safe space, where she can again open her heart. Because she is devoted to loving, she enters each interaction with others with an open heart, knowing that if her pain and fears are triggered, she can lovingly manage them, learn from them, and heal them. In choosing to take responsibility for her own feelings, Jodie is doing her part in creating a safe relationship space.

A safe relationship space is a glorious gift that we can give to ourselves and one another. As much as we may want this, we must accept that we have no control over whether or not our partner or others decide to join us on this path. We have total control over our own intent, and none over others. No matter how much we love those who are close to us, we cannot make them want to take responsibility for their own feelings. We cannot make them want to move off the path of fear onto the path of love and courage. All we can do is choose this for ourselves and hope others will join us.

Conflict Resolution

Healthy conflict resolution is vital for creating a safe relationship space. How we choose to handle conflict can foster or destroy the safe relationship space.

There are four possible outcomes in conflict:

- **Win-lose resolution:** when one person dominates and the other complies, giving themselves up.
- **Nonresolution:** when both people are trying to have their way, and both are resisting being controlled by the other.
- **Individual resolution:** when each person disengages from the conflict because there is no safe space in which to explore it. Each person decides how to take care of themselves.

- **Win-win resolution:** when both people have their own and the other's highest good at heart. New learning occurs naturally when both are learning about their own and the other's good reasons for feeling and behaving the way they do. This opens the door for win-win conflict resolution, where neither person feels they are compromising their integrity.

If our wounded self attempts to control during a conflict, we will destroy the safe relationship space and be unable to reach a healthy, win-win resolution. The wounded self has entirely different goals in conflict than the loving adult. The wounded self wants to win or not rock the boat, be in control, and not be controlled.

In a conflict with another, the wounded self believes one or more of the following:

- I know I am right, and I just want to win.
- Whether I'm right or wrong, all that is important is winning.
- I need to win in order to know that I am in control. Staying in control makes me feel safe, which is more important to me than learning about loving.
- I want to have peace; therefore I won't rock the boat even if it means giving myself up.
- I need to make sure I am not controlled or taken advantage of by another.
- Resisting control is more important to me than learning about loving.

To the loving adult, learning about loving is much more important than winning, remaining silent, controlling, resisting, or being right. The loving adult knows that true safety lies in loving oneself and caring about others, not in controlling others.

The loving adult believes:

- Being loving to myself and to others, and learning more about myself through this conflict, is more important to me than being right or protecting myself against rejection or engulfment.

- This conflict is an opportunity to learn something, and I am willing to risk staying in it through the difficulties in order to learn.

- I want to find a resolution that works well for both of us without requiring either of us to give ourselves up.

- If it is most important to another to win, remain silent, be right, protect against pain, be in control, or resist being controlled, I am willing to walk away from this conflict, leaving it unresolved, and take loving care of myself.

When you are in conflict with another, there are only two actions that can create and maintain a safe relationship space:

1. Move into an intent to learn about yourself and your partner.
2. Lovingly disengage from the conflict.

Being Open to Learning during Conflict

What does "being open to learning during conflict" mean? It means:

- You are committed to the process of learning about yourself and your partner.
- You are open to a win-win resolution rather than attempting to impose your will on your partner. You are devoted to the highest good of all.
- You believe that both you and your partner have good reasons for your feelings and behavior.
- You are willing to speak your total truth about your feelings and behavior without blaming or judging your partner for them.
- You are willing to hear your partner's total truth without blame or judgment about his or her feelings and behavior.
- You are available to offer physical and emotional comfort if your partner is in pain and is available for your help in managing the pain. Sometimes letting your partner know that he or she isn't alone, that you are here with your love, can open the door to learning, healing, and conflict resolution.
- You are willing to feel the pain of your loneliness and heartache if your partner shuts you out or tries to control you. You accept your helplessness over your partner's intent, and you do not attempt to control in the face of rejection or engulfment.

- You are willing to lovingly disengage from the discussion if your partner is not open to learning rather than attempting to control him or her.
- You are willing to lose your partner rather than losing yourself by compromising your personal integrity.
- You are not invested in the outcome of the conflict. If you attempt to explore a conflict and are invested in the outcome, you will try to control it. Learning and resolution cannot occur in a controlling environment. The way to be unattached to the outcome is to do your own six-step Inner Bonding process before attempting to resolve the conflict so that you can discover how to take care of yourself if your partner doesn't open to learning with you. Once you know you will be OK no matter what the outcome, you can approach the conflict without an agenda.

Once again, "partner" refers to anyone you are in a relationship with: mate, friend, relative, coworker, and so on.

If you have not completed your own inner work around a particular conflict before attempting to explore it with another, there is a good possibility that you will not be able to maintain a safe relationship space. It is very easy to become frustrated unless you are truly uninvested in the outcome.

Lovingly Disengaging

Disengaging without anger or blame allows you to care for yourself and creates the space for you to keep your heart open. Disengaging is not about controlling or changing another person's behavior or withdrawing and punishing the other person. It is about keeping your heart open while walking away from a conflict or a negative interaction. When you choose compassion for your loneliness, heartache, heartbreak, and helplessness over the other person, and are kind, gentle, tender, caring, and understanding with your core pain, you will keep your heart open.

For example, if your partner is yelling at you or shaming and blaming you, you might gently and lovingly say: "It hurts me when you yell at me. I really want to discuss this issue with you, so I'll be back in half an hour and see if we can talk." Then you need to leave the interaction with compassion for yourself, do your own Inner Bonding work to soothe your feelings, and check back in half an hour to see if your partner is open to learning with you. If you leave with anger and blame, however, you are attempting to control your partner. You are withdrawing rather than disengaging. Disengaging is about taking care of yourself with compassion for your own pain, not about controlling the other person by punishing them with your withdrawal of love.

Learning to lovingly disengage is a challenge, not because it is hard in itself, but because most people find it hard to let go of control. I encourage you to remember to ask your spiritual guidance for help in accepting your lack of control over another person, and in moving into compassion for yourself.

It is a great comfort to remember that whatever is loving to you will also be loving to your partner, even if they don't think so in the moment. Your loving behavior toward yourself gives your partner the opportunity to take responsibility for his or her own feelings and behavior.

As you can see, a safe relationship space is created only when both people have an intent to learn. However, we cannot force our partner to be open to learning. Attempting to control them further damages the safety of the relationship space. The loving action you can take is to pray for your partner to receive spiritual help in opening, and then do your own Inner Bonding process.

It is often valuable to have a third person, such as a therapist, facilitator, or knowledgeable friend, present to facilitate conflict resolution. No matter how sophisticated you may be with personal growth and conflict resolution, it is difficult to see yourself clearly when conflict arises. A third, neutral person can be invaluable in maintaining the safe relationship space.

The idea that we should be able to do this by ourselves is completely false, and prevents many people from seeking the help they need to resolve conflicts. Often within one or two sessions, I can help two people—a couple, business partners, siblings, a parent and adolescent or adult child, or friends—clearly understand the system that is keeping them stuck in conflict. It is often a huge relief for these people to see what they are each doing to create their unsafe relationship system. Organizations and nations bring in mediators for this very reason. This works wonderfully well when both parties or all concerned want to learn and reach a win-win resolution.

If Your Partner Isn't Onboard with Learning

What if your partner is not interested in learning with you? What if your partner has no interest in personal or spiritual growth? Does this mean you have to leave the relationship? No! As I stated earlier, if you are willing to do your own learning, you can maintain a satisfying relationship even if your partner is not open to learning.

While you will not have a safe relationship space, as long as you are creating a safe inner space, you can fill yourself with love and share it with your partner. As long as you are willing to disengage and take care of yourself in the face of your partner's controlling behavior, you can be happy in the relationship. Your happiness does *not* depend on your partner being open to learning. You both might share many things that are important to you, such as parenting, activities, values, and fun. You do not have to give these up just because your partner is not open to learning with you. As long as your relationship is not physically or emotionally abusive, it may be in your highest good to stay and take loving care of yourself rather than leave and look for a more open person.

Often only one partner seeks my help, because the other is not interested. However, when one partner learns to take full responsibility for his or her own feelings and behavior, the system changes. It has to change when one partner changes. Of course, you can't know whether it will change for the better or the worse, but my experience is that when one partner learns to take loving care of themselves and stops trying to control the other, the relationship often improves. Frequently, the closed partner now feels safe enough to open and even seek help for themselves.

Changing an Unsafe System

Often clients seek my help because they are very unhappy with their relationships. As we begin to work with Inner Bonding, a common and deep fear usually comes up: "What if I do this work, but my partner doesn't? What will happen to our relationship?" I tell them the odds are about fifty-fifty: there is a 50 percent chance that the other person will eventually join them on the path of love, and a 50 percent chance that the other person will move even further away. I tell them that until they are willing to lose their partner rather than continue to lose themselves, they will probably not find the courage to persist in healing their wounded self.

Amalia, a computer programmer in her mid-forties, was at the point of ending her twenty-year marriage when she discovered Inner Bonding through one of my books. Her husband, Eduardo, a landscape designer, was distant, uncommunicative, and occasionally violent with their adolescent children. In addition, he was constantly angry with her over her lack of sexual desire for him. The wounded, needy part of him wanted to fill his inner emptiness through sex. Amalia would often give in to avoid his anger, but she felt miserable about it. She could not see a way out of her unhappiness other than divorce.

Amalia started attending Inner Bonding workshops and intensives. She joined our online community and received the support she needed in her Inner Bonding practice. She soon realized that she had been a caretaker throughout her marriage, taking responsibility for Eduardo's feelings rather than for her own.

Shortly after starting to practice Inner Bonding, Amalia set a firm, loving limit with Eduardo: "I will not have sex with you unless we are emotionally connected and you are in a place of personal power instead of acting like a needy little boy. I am not turned on by needy little boys. I am turned on by a man who is open and caring about himself and me." She suggested that he attend one of my workshops to learn Inner Bonding.

To her great surprise, he did. Eduardo not only attended a workshop, he attended an intensive and joined Amalia on the journey to heal their wounded selves. Today Eduardo and Amalia have a completely new relationship. They take responsibility for their own feelings, which creates a safe relationship space, where they can share their love and truth with each other. As a result, they have achieved a depth of emotional intimacy they had never known before with each other—and their sex life is flourishing!

When Amalia decided to embark on the path of love and courage, she had to be willing to let go of the outcome. She needed to accept that she had no control over whether Eduardo would stay on the path of fear and continue to seek control or join her on the new path and learn about loving. She had to be willing to lose him rather than continue to lose herself.

The Path of Love and Courage

It takes great courage to change an unsafe relationship system. When you have been on the caretaking end of the system, it takes courage to stay steadfast in caring for yourself. Many people like it when someone gives themselves up to be their caretaker, and they may get angry and judgmental when you start to take care of yourself. Your partner, children, parents, and friends may tell you that you are no longer loving. As you start to set loving limits with them, you may hear about how selfish you are.

Sharon, one of my clients, finally learned to take care of herself instead of caretaking everyone else in her family. After setting some long-needed limits with two of her grown daughters, Sharon received the following letter from her husband, from whom she was separated:

"Sharon, when I think about you, I think about a person who, during the time we were together, was often able to stay loving no matter what else was going on. This person could love me and the kids, not just when we were also being loving, but even at those frequent times when we were not returning that love.

"I know that person often felt lonely and wondered what was wrong. I know she sometimes lost herself, and that her openness was taken advantage of. I know that she often ended up feeling depleted. Unfortunately, I did not value her and rarely expressed my love, and I am sad about that." (Her husband had been saying for years that he was sad about not expressing his love, yet nothing had ever changed. These were not new words or realizations, but, according to Sharon, the same old thing.) "Yet in the face of not getting the love and support she desired and deserved, she didn't lose her ability to love openly for a long, long time. That person is no longer with us, and we all miss her."

Upon receiving this letter, Sharon decided to move ahead with divorcing her husband. She saw that despite his seemingly loving words, he could not see her as a loving person as long as she was being loving to herself instead of caretaking others. She saw that he wanted desperately to pull her back into the old system rather than taking emotional responsibility for himself and supporting his grown daughters in learning to take emotional responsibility for themselves. Rather than expressing love for who Sharon was becoming, he attempted to undermine her path, hoping to pull her back into their old system.

It is sad that truly loving behavior is so often called selfish, while caretaking behavior, which is manipulative and avoids responsibility for oneself, is called loving. It is one of the crazy-making ways in which our society attempts to maintain control: teaching us that loving behavior toward oneself is selfish and unloving behavior toward oneself is loving. Our society's ideal of love is not love, but control through caretaking. Self-love is not selfish. As I stated earlier, the real definition of selfishness is being so self-centered that you expect others to give themselves up for your needs. In other words, you are selfish when you choose to be a taker and expect others to take responsibility for your feelings. When they don't, you tell them they are selfish for taking care of their own feelings and needs instead of yours. How turned around can things get?

It takes equally great courage to move out of the taker role in an unsafe relationship system. Often the caretaker has a deep need to feel needed and becomes threatened when the taker begins to assume responsibility for himself or herself. The caretaker may feel unloved and rejected if you move onto the path of love and courage, and may eventually become angry with you for attempting to change the system. If the caretaker's whole identity is tied up with being needed by others, he or she may look for another person to caretake.

Randolph, forty-one, consulted me because his anger was out of control. He had been arrested for threatening a waitress and spent the night in jail. Big and well-built, Randolph was a powerful and successful businessman. He was also a taker. He demanded that everyone—his wife, Katie, their children, and his employees—cater to his needs.

Because he was humiliated by having to spend a night in jail, Randolph was highly motivated to learn to manage his anger. He started working with Inner Bonding and discovered that anger was his way of intimidating others into taking care of his feelings and needs. As Randolph connected with his spiritual guidance and learned to be loving to himself, his need for others to cater to him gradually diminished.

Randolph's changes sent Katie into a tailspin. Her whole identity had been tied up in being needed. She had no sense of self. She completely defined herself through others' approval, which she had learned to get by caretaking. Now, instead of seeking out her caretaking, Randolph began to feel annoyed and manipulated by it.

Fortunately, Katie decided to work on her end of the system. She started having sessions with me, attended a workshop and an intensive, and devoted herself to learning to define her worth apart from being needed. Randolph and Katie have moved out of their stale and passionless relationship into a new relationship with each other—one filled with learning, passion, and fun.

Rocking the boat takes great courage for both the caretaker and the taker. You cannot do it alone. You cannot do it without the support of at least one other person, such as a friend, coach, facilitator, or therapist, or without a personal connection to your spiritual guidance. Without this connection, developed through practicing Inner Bonding or some other healing process on a daily basis, you may not have the strength to stay steadfast in the face of others' anger, blame, or rejection. When becoming strong enough to love and creating a safe relationship space becomes important to you, you will do the inner work necessary to create it at home, with friends, and at work.

6

How the Relationship Space Affects Sexuality

Many couples who love each other very much may think they do not have the same relationship problems as the couples in the previous chapter. They may think their problem—lack of desire or passion—is merely sexual. This is a common issue in committed relationships, and many couples find it mystifying: no matter what they do, they cannot seem to regain the passion they felt earlier in their relationship, even though the love is still there.

Sexual problems are often manifestations of relationship problems. Lack of sex in a relationship is rarely an isolated issue. More often it is a symptom of an unsafe relationship space.

Darryl and Leena

Darryl, a business analyst, and Leena, a children's clothes designer, had been married for thirty-two years when they consulted with me. Their two adult daughters were doing well on their own, and both were quite successful in their work. They had been to numerous therapists for help with their marriage but were still feeling disconnected from each other and had no sex life.

Leena came from a background of much neglect, along with physical abuse at the hands of both parents, and had deep abandonment and engulfment issues. Darryl had come from a household with a mentally ill mother who was physically violent with him and a father who was highly critical, and he too had deep abandonment and engulfment issues.

Darryl and Leena loved each other, but when I met them, they hadn't made love in a few years. The problem was that they were rarely connected enough for Leena to feel like making love, and Darryl was not at all happy about this.

It was quickly evident that neither Darryl nor Leena had a loving adult capable of creating inner safety, so the relationship space felt unsafe to both of them. Each was afraid of the other's anger, blame, judgments, and withdrawal. Each blamed the other's controlling behavior for their lack of connection, and neither was aware of their own anger and blame. They believed they were just reacting to the other's unloving behavior.

Both Darryl and Leena were treating themselves as they had been treated by their parents and then projected on to each other their own self-abandoning behavior. Fortunately, both were open to healing the relationship, so they both plunged into learning and practicing Inner Bonding.

It took time for each of them to become aware of their own behavior, which was creating their unsafe system. It took time for both Leena and Darryl to become aware of the anger and blame in their voices, because neither of them was overtly angry or blaming. It was all in their energy—their tone of voice. Our intent will always be betrayed in our energy. Even though each wanted to believe they were open to learning, their intent to control was evident in their voices, and they were sensitive and reactive to each other's angry and blaming energy. As long as they were avoiding responsibility for their pain and blaming each other, there was no way for them to feel safe.

Through their devotion to their Inner Bonding practice and taking responsibility for their own feelings, including speaking up with an intent to learn when the other was harsh and blaming, their system gradually shifted. Leena learned to say to Darryl, "You seem angry, and it's scaring me. I'd like to understand what's going on," and then lovingly disengage if Darryl wasn't open with her. Darryl learned to say, "This blaming feels hurtful to me. Can we talk about what's happening?" and to also lovingly disengage if Leena wasn't open. They learned to honor their own sensitivity to each other's energy and believe each other when they felt scared or hurt, rather than denying their controlling energy. As a result, the relationship space became safe enough for them to start making love again. At first it was sporadic, but gradually their sex life improved to the point that both were happy with it.

Each had to decide to be willing to be hurt rather than staying closed and protected against their fears of rejection and engulfment. This isn't an easy decision to make, yet for them, it was life changing.

The same was true for me. When I decided that I was willing to be hurt rather than to keep closing my heart to protect against pain, my ability to stay open and loving skyrocketed. I was able to make this decision as a result of my Inner Bonding practice. I now know that I can lovingly manage any pain, which means that through my Inner Bonding practice, I became strong enough to love.

Helga and Ricardo

Helga, a jewelry designer, and Ricardo, a chiropractor, have been married for almost twenty years. They love each other deeply, yet Helga often feels very lonely with Ricardo. She complains to him that he doesn't connect with her from his heart. She complains that throughout their marriage, Ricardo has been after her for sex, but that she is often not turned on to him. Helga and Ricardo struggle with a prevalent relationship issue: he sees sex as a means to connect with her, but she is not turned unless they are already emotionally connected.

Helga has often used her past pain to connect with Ricardo, insisting that he listen to her for hours while she cries and releases her pain. Being a caretaker, Ricardo often complies, but, feeling controlled and pulled on, he withholds on the feeling level. He is present physically but not emotionally. Helga is also a caretaker and tries to be there for Ricardo about his work problems, even when she is not interested in them. Similarly, she has sex when she is not turned on. She then resents the fact that even though she has given herself up to please him, he still does not connect with her on a feeling level the way she would like him to.

Ricardo comes from a fairly loving family background, but one in which he learned to be a caretaker for his mother, who was lonely because his father was often gone on business. Ricardo became his mother's "little man," the person she turned to for solace. She would often sigh and say, "I don't know what I would do without you." Ricardo learned to see himself as a hero, the good guy who comes upon the scene to save the day. His worth became tied up in being a savior. However, with Helga he doesn't feel like the good guy, because no matter what he does, she never seems to be happy. What worked with Ricardo's mother does not work with Helga. As a result, Ricardo often feels resistant to connecting emotionally with Helga.

As an infant, Helga was put up for adoption and spent the first six months of her life completely alone and neglected, awaiting adoption. Her fear of abandonment and her deep loneliness, helplessness, and heartbreak are activated when Ricardo is not emotionally available to her. Because she never learned to compassionately embrace her core painful feelings and give her infant within what she never received, she becomes controlling, pulling on Ricardo with her pain, her blame, and her anger. Ricardo, for his part, never learned to compassionately embrace his loneliness and heartache when Helga pulls on him and makes him responsible for her pain. Sometimes he gives in, listening to her half-heartedly, and sometimes withdraws. Helga's pulling and Ricardo's giving in or withdrawing creates an unsafe and unsatisfying relationship system.

As with most couples, Helga and Ricardo are acutely aware of what the other is doing to create the unsafe system, yet both are completely unaware of their own participation in it. Each points the finger at the other and says, "You are the problem." Helga tells Ricardo, "If only you would connect with my feelings and open to your own instead of pacifying me or shutting me out, I would feel connected with you and turned on. Stop making this all about me, and look at yourself." Ricardo tells Helga, "If only you stopped blaming me for your pain and pulling on me to fix you, I could feel connected with you. I'm tired of you always being in pain and it always being my responsibility to make you feel better, and I'm tired of being rejected sexually."

Both are right, yet neither is right. Each is right about what the other is doing, but mistaken to assume the responsibility is one-sided. Both people must take responsibility for themselves in order for the relationship space to become safe and satisfying.

When Helga opened to learning about her end of the system, she discovered that when she feels shut out by Ricardo—when he listens half-heartedly or withdraws—it touches into the deep and terrifying loneliness and helplessness of her infancy. She learned that she doesn't have to wait for Ricardo to rescue her terrified inner child: she can nurture the infant she was by imagining picking her up and holding her with deep love and compassion. When she lovingly acknowledges and holds her own inner child, she no longer needs Ricardo to take care of her feelings.

As for Ricardo, he discovered that when Helga pulls on him and hands him her inner child to comfort, he gives in or resists rather than tuning into the heartache of being made responsible for her feelings. Because he doesn't speak up and say that he is feeling pulled on and lonely and doesn't want the responsibility for Helga's feelings, his own inner child feels abandoned by him and wants to be rescued by a sexual connection.

Ricardo also discovered that much of his identity and worth were tied up in being the hero and taking care of others rather than in taking responsibility for his feelings and defining his worth. Because Ricardo made his worth dependent on Helga's happiness, he was often resentful toward her for being unhappy. When she didn't see him as a hero, Ricardo withheld his feelings and his presence from her as a form of punishment.

Ricardo decided to work on creating an identity separate from being a caretaker. He also decided to gently speak his truth to Helga when he was feeling pulled on and to open to learning with her, rather than giving in or resisting and then getting back at her in subtle ways. Helga decided to pick up her own inner child and comfort her rather than continuing to pull on Ricardo to do it. As a result, their unsafe relationship system is slowly healing. Both of them are feeling pleased and hopeful at being able to change the negative patterns that have existed for so many years, and both of them find themselves far more available to the sharing of love. They are happy to see what they each can do to create a loving flow between them. And Helga finds that her sexual feelings are more readily available to her (and to Ricardo) as a result of the changes in their system.

Helga and Ricardo exemplify the most common sexual problems in committed relationships. Ricardo tended to use sex addictively to feel worthy and connected, while Helga was rarely turned on. In my work with couples, I have found that these two issues, sexual addiction and a lack of sexual desire for the partner, plague many loving and committed relationships.

Sexual Addiction

Sexual addiction is like any other addiction. It is a form of controlling behavior that uses something or someone to fill you up or take away your pain. There are many levels of sexual addiction: the level depends upon the frequency and intensity with which you use sex addictively.

Are you sexually addicted? Checking one of the statements below may indicate a very mild sexual addiction, depending upon which one you checked; checking many of them suggests a moderate or severe sexual addiction. Mark the ones that apply to you:

☐ I (occasionally) (frequently) use sex to feel good about myself.

☐ I (occasionally) (frequently) use sex to fill up the emptiness within myself.

☐ I (occasionally) (frequently) use sex to take away my aloneness.

☐ I (occasionally) (frequently) use sex to take away my anxiety or tension.

☐ I (occasionally) (frequently) have trouble concentrating on other things due to my preoccupation with sex.

☐ I think about sex most of the time.

☐ My sexuality is my identity.

☐ I have an intense need for sex with my partner. If my partner doesn't want to have sex with me, I get angry or withdrawn.

☐ When I desire sex, I don't really care about my partner's feelings or desires. I just want it, and I feel justified in going after it.

☐ I believe my partner owes me sex.

☐ I sacrifice important parts of my relationship for sex. My sexual needs are more important to me than relationship needs.

☐ My sexual needs and my reaction when I do not get what I want sexually are interfering with my relationship with my partner.

☐ I have a compulsive need for sex with many partners.

☐ The pursuit of sex makes me careless of my own welfare and that of others.

☐ I am chronically preoccupied with sexual fantasies.

☐ I am promiscuous.

☐ I compulsively masturbate.

☐ I have a compulsive need to masturbate while viewing pornography.

☐ I feel compelled to participate in Internet sex.

☐ I am a voyeur.

☐ I am an exhibitionist.

☐ I feel controlled by my sexual desires.

☐ The only time I feel powerful is when I am imposing sex on someone.

☐ I am sexually attracted to children.

☐ I act out sexually with children.

☐ I force people to have sex with me.

☐ Hurting others turns me on sexually.

☐ Being hurt by others turns me on sexually.

As you can see, there are many different kinds and degrees of sexual addiction. Like any addiction, it comes from the wounded self, trying to find a way to have control over feeling safe and worthy. Sexual addiction, as well as any other addictions you may have, will heal as you develop your loving inner adult's capacity to manage your core existential painful life feelings.

The most common form of sexual addiction in a committed relationship is when one partner uses sex to feel filled, validated, or loved, or to relieve tension or anxiety. This person becomes needy and demanding, often resorting to anger or withdrawal when their partner doesn't want sex. This behavior can exacerbate another common problem: a lack of sexual desire. The person on the other end is generally turned off by their partner's neediness. After all, demanding and needy energy is not very attractive, erotic, or loving. Here's a common scenario:

George: Come on, honey, it's been over a week, and I'm really horny.

Martha: I just don't feel like it. It's late, and I'm tired.

George: You're always tired. Come on, you'll get into it. You know you will. I've got a big day tomorrow, and I need a good night's sleep. Come on.

George does not care about what Martha wants or how she feels. He is just concerned with what he wants, which is one of the symptoms of sexual addiction: a lack of concern for your partner's needs and desires.

I've worked with men who were very sexually needy in one relationship. They left that relationship, ended up with a woman who was more sexually needy than they were, and found themselves turned off by it.

Take Scott, for example. Scott was in his thirties and was married to Melinda. Scott and Melinda came to me for help because Scott was unhappy that she was rarely turned on sexually. He would get angry and distant when his sexual needs weren't met, while Melinda, feeling pressured by Scott's demands, withdrew more and more. In addition, she was dealing with past issues of sexual abuse from her father, and Scott's demands were triggering her old fear and pain. She felt unloved and used by Scott, just as she had felt unloved and used by her father.

Scott finally left her and before long met up with another woman, who was very sexual. Delighted, he jumped into this new relationship. Soon, however, he was back working with me, complaining that for some unknown reason, he was no longer feeling very sexual. His intense sexuality—the sexual "needs" that he claimed were just part of being "a normal, red-blooded male"—seemed to have disappeared.

As we explored the issue, it became apparent that Scott's new girlfriend, Karen, was very sexually demanding and would become hurt and agitated if he wasn't turned on by her.

Scott realized that the tables had turned: Karen was behaving with him as he had behaved with

Melinda. He felt turned off by Karen's neediness and used by her the same way Melinda had felt used by him! He saw that what he thought were his sexual needs were really a means of control. He had wanted control over Melinda's desire for him, and Karen wanted control over his desire for her. Scott was stunned when he realized that his loss of his sex drive was really about resisting control, just as Melinda's had been. He had been so sure that his sexual "needs" were purely biological!

I have found this over and over: what a man or woman thinks is a strong sex drive is often a craving for power. More than wanting sex itself, the person wants control over getting sex, control over the other's sexual desire. This is even more apparent with those who are constantly seeking new sex partners, yet lose interest in the person after the first sexual encounter (or even before). Their pleasure lies in the conquest and the resulting sense of power and validation rather than in the sex itself. I have worked with both men and women who complained to me that although they find themselves constantly seeking new sex partners, they rarely enjoy the sex act. They don't realize they are using sexual conquest in the same way another person might use making money: to stave off pain and fear and gain a sense of worth through power over others.

Our society is rampant with sexual addiction. The media play on it by promoting products that are "sexy." Ads show how a man's or a woman's desirability is enhanced by cars, clothing, and jewelry. These ads work because so many people define themselves externally, by their sexual desirability.

Lack of Sexual Desire

Lack of a sex drive is another huge problem in our society. In at least 80 percent of the heterosexual couples I work with who have sexual problems, the woman lacks sexual desire for her partner, while in about 20 percent the man lacks sexual desire for his. There are numerous causes for the absence of sexuality in a relationship. Some of them are physical, such as recovering from childbirth, shifting hormones during the menstrual cycle or during menopause, or exhaustion due to overwork or child-rearing. If you are a woman experiencing a general lack of sexual desire, you might want to check with your doctor. A physical cause for a man might be low testosterone.

After physical causes are ruled out, there are four common emotional causes for a lack of sexual desire in a committed relationship:

1. Lack of emotional intimacy. Many people need to feel loved and connected with their partner before they want to make love. If you and your partner do not spend intimate time together outside of the bedroom, your sexual relationship may lack spark.

2. No safe relationship space in which to bring up problems between you. If one or both of you are not open to learning when conflict comes up,

the flow of love, and therefore of sexual energy, diminishes. If, when you bring up an issue, your partner responds with anger, blame, defensiveness, resistance, withdrawal, or inattentiveness, you will not have a safe space in which to resolve these issues. This lack of safety creates a lack of loving energy, which can translate into a lack of sexual desire.

3. Caretaking: giving yourself up to your partner's demands. Perhaps you have never recognized that your sexual desire may be deadened by caretaking, but I have found that the more a person gives themselves up in any area of a relationship, the less sexual desire they feel. If you allow your partner to control you in even minor areas of your relationship, it may be affecting your sex life.

4. Your partner has a sexual addiction that makes you feel used rather than loved during sex. It may be difficult for you to feel attracted to your partner when he or she is operating from a sexual addiction. When you are being pulled on by a sexually addicted partner, you may feel objectified rather than loved. Your partner wants to use you rather than love you, and that is not a turn-on to most people.

Someone who is operating from a sexual addiction comes to his or her partner like a child, needy for attention and validation. One of the major reasons there are so many turned-off wives in our culture (research indicates that 48–54 percent of married women do not experience sexual desire for their partners) is that heterosexual women are turned on by men who are personally empowered, not men who behave like needy little boys attempting to get their needs met through sex. Most women need to feel emotionally safe to desire sex, and a needy or demanding partner, or a partner who gets angry if the woman doesn't want it, creates emotional distance and an unsafe relationship space.

Some years ago, Oprah Winfrey had writer Christine Ferraro and a number of couples on her show to discuss this issue. One husband described how he buys his wife flowers, draws her bath, and lights candles in the hope that she will feel loved enough to want to make love. The wife disclosed that as soon as her husband drew her a bath, she cringed inwardly, because she knew what his agenda was. He was not offering her a gift or sharing his love. She felt manipulated her into giving him the sex he wanted and was turned off. As long as her husband tried to get something from her rather than truly giving something to her, she did not feel loved by him or emotionally connected with him.

If you have a history of sexual abuse, you may feel very conflicted with a partner who is sexually addicted. You may find yourself responding physically to your partner, yet emotionally you may feel repulsed. When this happens, it is because your past experiences with a sexual addict are coloring your present-day responses.

Whatever the cause of a lack of sexual desire, it will not get resolved without a safe relationship space. Let's go back to George and Martha. George wants sex so he can have a good night's sleep. He does not care that Martha doesn't feel like making love. If Martha were taking good care of herself, she would compassionately feel her loneliness when George doesn't care about her. She would let him know that her heart aches and she does not feel sexual when he is needy rather than loving. Rather than give herself up, she would speak her truth and attempt to learn with George about why he is pushing her to do something she doesn't want to do.

George could also attempt to learn both about himself and about Martha. He could explore why having sex is more important to him than caring about Martha and respecting her wishes. What does sex mean to him? Does he get his sense of worth and lovability through it? Does he feel manly, attractive, and desirable only when Martha wants to have sex with him? George could also open to understanding the heartache Martha feels when he is unloving with her. By choosing not to bully Martha sexually, George would be taking full responsibility for his own feelings and needs rather than making Martha responsible for them.

Through staying open to learning, George and Martha can begin to resolve their sexual problems.

Learning to create a safe relationship space is the key to a fulfilling intimate and connected relationship.

Sometimes in a relationship, one partner is addicted to connection while the other partner is addicted to being sexually desired. The insatiable longing for connection or for being desired, and the feeling of powerlessness over getting what each person wants, leads to controlling behavior, thus creating the unsafe relationship space. Until each partner does the inner work necessary to connect with, define, and value themselves, they will continue to pull on each other to fill the emptiness within.

Joseph and Tess

Joseph and Tess are a good example of a couple who managed to move out of the power struggle over sex that was wreaking havoc with their relationship. When they consulted with me, they had been married for four years. Joseph, thirty-three, is a high-powered attorney, and Tess, twenty-eight, works as a midwife. When they first met, they fell madly in love, and sex was great for about six months. Then slowly the sex dwindled. Tess found herself more and more resistant to it, and Joseph was constantly angry about the lack of it. They had tried various forms of therapy, including making contracts to make love twice a week, but nothing was working, and Tess was seriously considering leaving the marriage. She could no longer stand the pressure Joseph was putting on her. They consulted with me at this point.

It soon became evident that Joseph was sexually addicted. Not only was he using sex to get release from the pressure of his job, but he had given Tess the responsibility of defining his worth. It was her job to make him feel worthy and attractive by desiring him sexually and having sex with him. The more Joseph acted like a needy, controlling child and pulled on Tess for sex, the more turned off and lonely she felt.

While Tess did not want the responsibility of defining Joseph's worth, she was also not taking responsibility for her own core pain: the loneliness and heartbreak she was feeling as a result of Joseph's anger at her.

Since Tess loved Joseph and sex with him had been so great at one time, she did not understand why she was not turned on to him. In fact, sex was still great during the rare times they made love. It wasn't the sex itself that was the problem, it was getting to the point of having sex. Tess felt there was something wrong with her because she didn't desire sex with Joseph. She became defensive about her lack of sexual feelings, and when Joseph approached her, she rejected him harshly, increasing the distance between them. Joseph felt rejected not only because Tess did not desire sex with him, but because of the harsh way she said no.

Fortunately, they were both motivated to do their inner work. I worked individually with each of them, facilitating the Inner Bonding process. Tess learned that when she did not compassionately attend to her core pain, she did not feel her sexuality. When her inner child felt abandoned by her, Tess could not access her sexual feelings. She also learned that she needed an emotional connection and a feeling of love before she felt turned on; when Joseph was needy and pulling on her, she did not feel loved, but felt disgusted with his demands. At these times, sex was the furthest thing from her mind.

Tess also learned that when she validated her own experience of feeling pulled on and compassionately attended to her own core pain, she did not have to respond harshly. She could respond by gently speaking her truth and opening to learning. She learned to say, with softness and warmth, "Honey, I'm feeling really pulled on, and it hurts my heart. I can't feel turned on when I feel this loneliness and heartache. Neediness is not a turn-on to me. I love you, and I want to feel turned on to you. Maybe we can talk about what you're feeling and why you are feeling needy."

Joseph learned to accept that when Tess experienced him as needy, he really was needy, and there was a good reason he felt that way. Joseph discovered that he spent most of his time in his head, completely ignoring his feelings, so his inner child often felt abandoned by him. He discovered that he often made others responsible for his worth by seeking their approval. He learned to dialogue with his spiritual guidance to define his own worth and lovability and discover what his inner child needed from him to feel safe and loved. He also found that he needed time to walk in nature after work and connect with himself; when he gave himself this time, he felt much less needy. He also learned that when Tess was harsh, instead of attending to his loneliness and heartache, he avoided it by pulling even more on Tess.

In addition, Joseph did some deep soul-searching about his true intent. Was it more important for him to have sex with Tess and have control over having sex with her, or was it more important to love her? After some resistance from his wounded self, he concluded that he really loved Tess and didn't want to lose her; he wanted to love her even if they never had sex again. This was a huge decision for him, and one that he did not make lightly. His wounded self saw the choice of love over control as losing, giving in, doing it Tess's way. When the wounded self stops trying to control, it feels as if it is losing the power struggle. As long as winning or losing, giving in or not giving in, was the issue, Joseph was stuck in the controlling system.

When it comes to loving, there is no such thing as losing or giving in, but since the wounded self is concerned with control rather than with loving, it cannot see things this way. Only when becoming a loving human being is more important to us than controlling can we relinquish the power struggle and give from the heart, with no expectations. Then we can reap the benefits of spiritually connected sex.

When Joseph finally made the choice to make love his highest priority, his energy toward Tess completely changed. His giving to her was no longer goal-oriented. Now he gave to her just because he loved her, and it felt good to give to her. It felt good to Tess too.

Within a week of Joseph's decision, Tess found herself initiating sex, something she had not done for a long time. Tess and Joseph gradually moved back into a passionate and satisfying sexual relationship. They may never have as much sex as Joseph would like, since he has a stronger sex drive than Tess, but the sex they have is extremely satisfying to both of them. Joseph no longer withdraws or gets angry when Tess doesn't want sex, which shows her she is loved for herself, not for the sexual gratification she provides.

Harv and Nancy

Harv called me for phone consultations because his wife, Nancy, threatened to leave him if he did not get some help.

"I must be all messed up with my sexuality. I constantly want sex with my wife, and she is fed up with it. When she won't have sex with me, I'm angry and sullen. I love my wife, and I don't want her to leave, but I can't seem to help myself. I'm very confused about all of this. Is it wrong to love your wife and want sex with her? Is it my problem or hers? Is there something wrong with her sexually that she doesn't want more sex with me?"

Harv filled me in on his background. He grew up with a highly judgmental and controlling father. It seemed that no matter how hard Harv worked in their factory and at school, it was never good enough for his father. As we worked together, it became apparent that Harv had learned his lessons well. His father's voice was constantly in his head, judging him for not working enough. He beat himself up mercilessly if he made a mistake, telling himself how inadequate he was: "You certainly messed that up." "You are such a jerk." "You never do anything right." "What's the matter with you?" "You're a loser, and you will always be a loser." His wounded self was totally in charge, trying to have control over getting him to do everything right in order to get others' approval.

Harv's ubiquitous self-judgment meant that his inner child felt constantly abandoned, which created intense aloneness and emptiness within him. This made him dependent upon others to fill him up and make him feel good.

As we worked together, Harv became aware of the knot of aloneness and emptiness in his stomach that he felt whenever he judged himself. He realized that whenever he felt this knot, he wanted to have sex to release the stress. As a child, he had learned to masturbate to release the stress he felt from his father's constant judgment of him. He became addicted to using orgasm as a way of managing his stress. Now, in his marriage, he was addicted to his wife releasing his tension. He believed that it was her job to provide this for him, since she was his wife.

Naturally, this did not lead Nancy to feel loved by him or attracted to him. In no uncertain terms, she told him that she felt used by him and was no longer willing to have sex unless there was emotional intimacy and connection between them. She told him she was turned off by his neediness and was unwilling to be a mere source of release.

Harv had not realized that his tension was being caused by his own self-judgments. He believed that it was caused by outside circumstances, such as problems at work or disapproval from other people. As he became more aware of his inner system, he saw that each time he judged himself, he felt that knot, and each time he felt the knot, he wanted sex to release it.

As we explored his beliefs about why it was so important to judge himself, Harv learned that he believed if he didn't work hard enough or he made mistakes, he was a bad person. He felt he needed to judge himself to get himself to work hard enough and avoid making mistakes in order to be a good person.

As long as Harv believed these things, he would judge himself to get himself to work harder and do things right. Through our work together, Harv learned to embrace his essential goodness—his caring, compassion, gentleness, and tenderness. He was able to see his wonderful qualities in his relationships with his small children, whom he dearly loved. When he learned to define his goodness internally, instead of externally through his work and performance, he gradually became able to let go of his self-judgments.

As a result of his Inner Bonding work, Harv is no longer using sex addictively. He approaches Nancy for sex only when he is feeling happy, peaceful, and loving. He has discovered that there is nothing wrong with Nancy's sexuality: she is wonderfully passionate when feeling loved rather than used!

Passion in Spiritually Connected Relationships

Remember what it's like when you fall in love? Everything is heightened: colors are brighter, laughter is deeper, passion abounds. Then, inevitably, our dual fears of being rejected or controlled are triggered, and the wounded self attempts to protect itself with controlling behavior. The unsafe relationship system is created.

The good news is that whenever two people who have previously shared fun, joy, and passion decide to create a safe relationship space, their feelings of passion can return—sometimes fairly quickly.

Ryan and Celine

Ryan and Celine fell madly in love with each other. Both had previously been in unhappy, passionless marriages and were delighted to discover that they were each capable of intensity and passion. They just couldn't seem to keep their hands off each other. Laughter abounded between them. Both were sure they had found their soul mate.

This lasted about a year, until they got married and moved in together. Within a few months, the power struggles started. Both Ryan and Celine are intelligent and highly verbal people. Both have strong opinions about how things should be done. Celine couldn't stand Ryan's poor eating habits. Ryan couldn't stand Celine's bossiness. Celine was outraged at how Ryan spent their money. Ryan felt smothered and controlled, and became resistant. In no time, not only had they lost their passion, but they found themselves having horrendous fights, replete with name-calling and occasionally even hitting. It got so bad that Ryan moved out and got his own apartment.

Neither Ryan nor Celine really wanted to end the relationship. They still loved each other and had fun together during those intermittent times when they weren't fighting. True, the sex had completely gone out of their relationship, but they could still laugh together. More important, both realized that their relationship offered them an opportunity to learn and grow. They each could see that they were doing the same things they had done in their previous relationships, and they were ready to break the pattern.

When they consulted with me, both Celine and Ryan deeply desired to heal the relationship, but each secretly believed that the problems were the other person's fault. Celine knew that if only Ryan would grow up and take responsibility for his health and indulgent spending, everything would be fine.

She believed that the real problem was Ryan being a resistant child instead of a responsible adult. On the other hand, Ryan knew that if only Celine would back off and stop trying to control him, everything would be fine. He believed that the real problem was Celine being a parental, controlling bitch. They were now completely unattracted to each other sexually, and both had grave doubts that they could regain their passion.

It didn't take long for Ryan and Celine to see their system. As they began to practice Inner Bonding, they were soon able to take their eyes off the other as the source of the problem and begin taking responsibility for themselves. Ryan confronted his resistance, his deep fears of being controlled, and his self-indulgent eating and spending. Celine confronted her intense need to be right and in control. She realized that anger was her primary way of avoiding feeling her loneliness when Ryan was emotionally unavailable and her helplessness when he was resistant.

After a few months of learning how to manage their core pain and create a safe relationship space, Ryan and Celine announced that they had made love—for the first time in a year! Furthermore, it was as it had been at the beginning: full of passion and fun. They were amazed and delighted to discover what powerful results they got from learning to take responsibility for themselves and creating a safe relationship space.

Tim and Ling

Tim and Ling had been married for fifteen years when they consulted with me. They sought help because Ling had just told Tim that she would no longer have sex with him.

Tim was furious. "She's my wife. How can she just decide not to have sex anymore? What does she expect me to do?"

"Tim, do you know why Ling doesn't want to have sex with you anymore?"

"Well, I know what she says. That she feels like an object, that I just want sex with her to feel 'validated.' She says she feels used, not loved, and she's tired of feeling like a prostitute."

"How do you feel about all that?"

"It's a bunch of crap! We're married! How can she feel like a prostitute?"

"So you don't understand her feelings."

"Oh, I understand, all right! She is just trying to control me. Women love to control men with sex. She is withholding sex from me to get what she wants. That's what all this is about."

"What do you think she wants?"

"She wants to make me be just like her and do things her way."

"So you don't believe what she is saying to you?"

"It's a bunch of crap!"

"Ling, how are you feeling about this?"

"Well, this is typical of how Tim responds to me. This is part of the problem. Sex seems more important to him than me and how I feel. I feel so discounted and so frustrated that he doesn't even want to try to understand how I feel."

"And how do you feel inside?"

"Sad. Lonely. I don't know how he expects me to feel turned on when he is so angry and makes light of what I feel. I've tried and tried to explain that I don't feel turned on when he just expects me to have sex and doesn't care how I feel. If I say no, he gets mad. He never tries to understand. I've given in for years just so he wouldn't be mad at me, but I can't do it anymore. I don't know if I'll ever feel like making love with him again. Right now the thought of it makes me sick."

"Ling, can you articulate what exactly turns you off?"

"I've thought about it a lot. It's like he comes to me empty and wants me to fill him up, and I'm tired of filling him up. It's worn me out. I feel like he has a big black hole inside that he doesn't know how to fill, so he wants me to fill it for him. He has nothing to give me. He just wants to take my love and my energy. It feels like getting me to have sex with him is all that matters. I always feel like everything he does, he does with the agenda of having sex. For him it's about getting sex, not loving me. He just wants to get me to fill his black hole."

"And what fills you? How do you get filled up inside?"

"Lots of ways. Being with our kids. Being in nature. Listening to music. Painting. Reading. Praying and talking with God."

"So you've decided that you will not make love with Tim until he comes to you without the black hole?"

"Right. I told him that until he comes to me filled with love, I will not make love with him."

Tim was not at all happy about this. When I mentioned sexual addiction, he went into vociferous denial, claiming that he was just a normal, red-blooded man who wanted sex with his wife. He refused to make another appointment and left angry. Ling decided to continue working with me by herself. She knew she needed to learn to take better care of herself and trust her feelings. She knew she needed support to deal with the difficult months to come. And she needed to learn to compassionately acknowledge and embrace her core painful feelings.

Two months later, Tim called and asked to have another appointment. This time he was a bit more open. He said he couldn't get the term "sexual addiction" out of his head, and he wanted to know more about it. We started to work with the emptiness inside him.

As Tim began to practice Inner Bonding, it was apparent that he was doing it to get Ling to make love to him again. He practiced it for months, but when Ling still refused to sex with him, he again became enraged. It was very difficult for him to understand that he was using Inner Bonding as a manipulative tool rather than as a means to becoming a more loving human being. Tim was still more devoted to having control over getting sex than being a loving person.

But because he was so miserable, he kept at it. A turning point came when Tim attended a five-day Inner Bonding Intensive. There he was confronted by one of the women participants about his "leaky" sexual energy. She told him she did not feel safe with him because she felt he was pulling on her for some kind of sexual validation.

Although she didn't feel he was coming on to her, she did feel that he wanted her to be attracted to him. Ironically, she used the same words Ling had used: "When I'm talking with you at breaks, I feel like you are a black hole waiting to be filled by someone. I feel pulled on to fill your black hole."

It had been easy for Tim to discount Ling's experience, but hearing the exact same thing from a stranger was life changing for him. He finally accepted that he was, indeed, sexually addicted. He started to practice Inner Bonding in earnest now, truly desiring to learn how to fill his black hole by connecting with himself and his spiritual guidance. He also began to attend Sex and Love Addicts Anonymous meetings.

Tim had much to heal, having experienced much rejection as a child. Early on he had learned to use anger to avoid his heartbreak, and in adolescence, he had learned to use sex to fill the emptiness created by the self-abandonment resulting from his fear of feeling his core pain.

Tim and Ling ended up not having sex for two years while each worked on their own end of their unsafe relationship system. One day, after I had not worked with them for a while, they had a session with me, and I could feel them smiling broadly over the phone. Ling spoke glowingly of how she now felt loved by Tim. She felt his genuine desire to love and connect with her rather than just get sex from her. She was surprised and delighted to discover that her early passion for Tim had returned in full force. She told me with awe in her voice that her body felt ready and available for sex most of the time when Tim approached her, and that she found herself approaching him far more often than she had at the beginning of their marriage. What had seemed like a hopeless situation was now healed.

Tim and Ling could easily have ended their relationship, concluding that there was no way to repair it. The only thing that really kept them together during those very difficult two years was not wanting to break up their family. One or both could have had affairs. Instead, they decided to do their individual inner healing work. And they are immeasurably glad they did.

Rona and Sy

When Rona and Sy came to see me, they had not had sex in three years. In fact, all sex had stopped three months after their wedding. Rona, who is a talented commercial artist, was no longer attracted to Sy, a stockbroker, yet she didn't know why. Both were physically attractive people in their mid-thirties, intelligent, articulate, and financially successful.

It soon became apparent that Rona and Sy were locked into an unsafe, codependent system. Rona would constantly pull on Sy for attention and validation. She would talk on and on, expecting him to be attentive to everything she had to say. She would get angry if his attention wandered. She wasn't at all interested in listening to him. Sy complied with Rona's wishes and was extremely attentive, yet nothing he did seemed to satisfy her.

I pointed out that each of them was making the other person responsible for their feelings. Rona needed constant validation from Sy, but even when she got it, it didn't make her happy or responsive to him. Sy was trying to control Rona's opinion of him by giving himself up to her need to talk and by taking responsibility for her feelings, hoping that if he did it "right," she would be attracted to him. Sy would end up feeling like a victim when Rona would get mad at him and refuse to make love. Rona didn't respect Sy because she was able to control him with her neediness and anger. She could not be turned on by a man she didn't respect. As a result, both partners felt unfulfilled.

Ironically (and this is often the case) the very thing Rona was trying to get from Sy (validation) was what she needed to give herself. And vice versa: the very thing Sy gave Rona (attention and care) was what he needed to give to himself. Fortunately, both were open to learning about taking responsibility for their own feelings and needs. Rona started spending time with herself, dialoguing with her inner child and her spiritual guidance. The more time she spent listening to herself and taking care of herself, the less she needed Sy to do these things for her. By meeting her own need for attention and compassion, she discovered that she was interested in listening to Sy.

Sy struggled with giving up his caretaking. He had been a caretaker his whole life, starting with his mother. Being needed by a woman was a big part of his identity and sense of worth. He was also very dependent on Rona's approval—and terrified of her anger. As Rona became more independent, Sy found himself feeling threatened by her not needing him anymore. The happier Rona became, the more miserable Sy was. Finally he came to grips with how much he felt like a victim, how dependent he was on Rona's approval, and how much he was abandoning himself. At this point, Sy really started doing his own Inner Bonding work. He started noticing and attending to his own feelings instead of taking responsibility for Rona's feelings.

It took a while for Rona and Sy's unsafe relationship system to change, but slowly fun and affection began to inch back into their relationship. Finally, after two years of working hard on themselves, Rona and Sy renewed their sexual relationship. Rona was amazed at the resurgence of her own desires. For a long time, she had assumed that she had married the wrong man and would never again feel turned on by Sy.

I have seen this countless times: doing one's own inner work and learning to take full responsibility for one's own feelings and needs generates a flow of loving energy that brings back the passion, fun, and joy we all seek with our partners.

Having sex is not a need. We can live without sex, and many people do remain celibate their whole lives. Sleep, food, water, air, love—these are needs. Sex is a desire. When two people become strong enough to love and create a safe relationship space, they will make love only when both desire it as a way to express their love for each other. When this is the case, sex becomes an entirely different experience than when the wounded self demands it. It becomes a spiritual experience. Spiritually connected sex is a sharing of universal energy, the life force that is within each of us and is a gift of Spirit. Sharing this creative energy through lovemaking is a delicious experience in a relationship. It can continue to be a delicious experience no matter how long you have been together.

In my many years of working with couples, I have discovered that any committed relationship, no matter how currently distant and dysfunctional, can become loving, provided both people are willing to take responsibility for their own feelings and the sexual attraction was there at the beginning, or within the first six months of the relationship. Any relationship that once had sexual passion can have it again, no matter how long it has been absent. But if there was no passion to begin with—if two people got married as friends and never felt a sexual spark—it is unlikely that passion will develop.

Sexual chemistry is a mysterious thing. Most of the time you either have it with someone or you don't. Some couples, as they become open to taking responsibility for their own feelings, discover that they are not suited to each other as lovers. They are just very good friends. Sometimes this is OK, because their companionship is more important to them than sexuality. Sometimes it is not OK, and they part as good friends, hoping to find passion in another relationship. Whatever the outcome, whether they stay together or move on, they are forever grateful they did the inner work necessary to become strong enough to love.

Passionate sexuality in long-term relationships comes from the spiritual connection between the partners. It is the outgrowth of creating a safe relationship space. It does not depend on looks or age. Passion deepens as love deepens. When two people are connected in this way, there is no need for multiple sexual partners. The appeal of one-night stands, casual sex, open marriage, and short-term affairs pales in the face of the richness, depth, satisfaction, and joy of spiritually connected sex.

7

Ingredients and Rewards of Safe Relationship Spaces

Now that you have seen how Inner Bonding works and how powerfully it can impact the lives of people who practice it, let's look more closely at exactly what creates a safe relationship space.

Compassion

Compassion is one of the most powerful energies there is. As with love, we don't generate it within ourselves: we open and invite it in from Spirit. When you consciously open to learning and invite Spirit into your heart, you are inviting in the energies of love and compassion.

Sometimes people ask me what compassion feels like. It is easier to define by the actions you take when it is guiding your choices than by the feeling itself. The actions of compassion are kindness, caring, tenderness, gentleness, and understanding.

While you might not know what compassion looks or feels like, we all know what kindness is. Instead of worrying about whether or not you feel compassionate, just choose to be kind, caring, tender, gentle, and understanding—with yourself and with others.

Imagine what your life would have been like if you had a parent who was deeply compassionate with you when you were hurting. Most of us didn't have this, but it is not too late. Now we have the opportunity to give this to ourselves and others.

Compassion is the opposite of judgment. When you choose compassion, you are in a loving adult state with a deep desire to learn about your wounded self, your core self, and the loving action toward yourself. Compassion creates a safe inner space and a safe relationship space; judgment destroys it. Think about how safe you feel when you spend time with someone who is truly compassionate about your feelings and behavior.

Compassion is not the same thing as feeling sorry for yourself or others. When you are feeling sorry for yourself, you are choosing to be a victim instead of learning about and taking responsibility for your feelings. Self-pity is the result of the wounded self's belief that your wounded feelings are caused by others or by outside events rather than by your own beliefs or behavior, and that others are responsible for taking care of your core painful feelings. While others can cause our painful existential feelings of life, we are still responsible for learning how to lovingly managing these feelings.

Sometimes you may think you are being compassionate with others when you being sympathetic, but sympathy is about feeling sorry for them. Feeling sorry for others is not helpful: it supports them in seeing themselves as victims. After a while, you may resent spending so much energy supporting and feeling sorry for others while not getting anything back (a sure sign that you have been caretaking). Or you get stuck in misery as you feel sorry for each other. There is no safe relationship space when you are supporting each other in being victims.

You need to have compassion for yourself before you can be truly compassionate with others. Often people who are caring are filled with compassion, but they immediately extend it to others before themselves. This leaves their inner child needy for loving attention. When you give compassion to others but not to yourself, it has strings attached: you are giving it in the hope that it will be given back to you. Consequently, compassion becomes another way to control, and the other person may feel pulled on rather than cared about.

When you have compassion for yourself, you are accepting the sacred privilege of validating your own feelings, knowing that they are a powerful inner guidance system. You trust that you have good reasons for all your feelings and behavior, and you open to learning about the underlying false beliefs that are fueling your wounded feelings. It is not compassionate to judge yourself, telling yourself that your feelings and behavior are wrong, bad, or stupid.

As you practice Inner Bonding, your caring and compassion will naturally extend to others. Your self-compassion and your compassion for your partner provide the basis for a safe relationship space.

There is another very important way that compassion creates a safe relationship space. When I learned to move into compassion for my loneliness and heartache the moment there was any negative energy coming towards me from another—anger, blame, judgment, or any type of attack—I discovered that I could extend that compassion to the wounded person who was attacking me. When I did, I found that I was surrounded with a warm, loving energy that repelled the negative energy of the attack.

For example, one day I was leaving the market with my shopping cart when a woman, in a hurry and not looking where she was going, banged into me as she entered the store. She immediately shot me an angry look and yelled, "Watch where you're going!" My stomach tightened as I felt the attack of her angry energy. I immediately moved into compassion for my own heart hurt and let my inner child know that she was not bad or wrong. Once I did, I looked at the woman, who seemed very hassled, smiled at her with kindness, and moved on. My compassion toward both myself and her released the tightness in my stomach, and I once again felt peaceful. The negative energy that she tried to dump on me found no home with me.

The energy of compassion is far more powerful than anger, judgment, or blame. Just as darkness cannot prevail when you turn on a light, so the darkness of attack cannot prevail against the powerful light of compassion. You will move into your personal power when you can remain compassionate with yourself and others in the face of attack. I believe that if we were each devoted to the daily practice of opening to compassion for our core painful feelings around others' negative energy, we would bring about the healing of our planet.

It is not easy to remember to open to compassion for your own feelings the moment you are attacked. It takes lots of practice to be in this moment—in the now—with your inner experience. This is the essence of Step One of Inner Bonding: choosing to be mindful of your feelings and your inner experience at all times. Learning to do this is well worth the effort. When I am able to maintain compassion in the face of attack, I end up feeling elated instead of devastated. My inner child feels safe when I am compassionately attentive to her core pain instead of reacting to others' controlling behavior. Often it so thoroughly disarms the other person that they stop attacking and open to learning.

The more you open to compassion for your core painful feelings at the first sign of attack, the better you will get at doing it. As we practice Inner Bonding, opening to compassion for ourselves and others, we begin to see the light within, our true soul self. This enables us to see the beautiful essence in everyone and experience our oneness with each other, which is vital for healing the darkness on our planet. We cannot do harm to ourselves, others, animals, or our planet when we deeply experience our oneness with all of life.

Empathy

Empathy is the ability to feel and deeply understand another's feelings. Many people are born with the ability to feel empathy, but some people put a lid on it because they don't want to be affected by others' pain. Other people may be born without this ability or shut it down so early in their life that it becomes inaccessible to them. An inability to feel empathy is one of the main characteristics of a narcissistic personality disorder.

Being able to empathize with your partner is vitally important for creating a safe relationship space. Knowing that your partner truly understands your feelings and can feel along with you creates a depth of intimacy that's not otherwise possible.

Like compassion, empathy isn't the same as sympathy. Sympathy can come from the wounded self in the form of pity, and, as I've stated, might enable the other person to feel like a victim. "Poor thing" might encourage "poor me," which is never helpful.

Nor is empathy the same thing as compassion. People can express the kindness and caring of compassion without actually feeling the other person's feelings. When we truly feel another's feelings, we will naturally have compassion, but showing compassion doesn't mean we are experiencing empathy.

Mirroring

Mirroring is another vital ingredient in creating a safe relationship space, and it is a great gift we can give each other. Mirroring is reflecting to another person their essence, who they really are in their core self.

When we were little, we needed mirroring from our parents in order to know our innate lovability and worth. Unfortunately, since many of our parents did not know their own core self, they couldn't see ours. As a result, we grew up believing we are our wounded selves, not knowing who we really are.

In my five-day intensives, we give the gift of mirroring to one another. After people have revealed their wounded selves, they are astounded to hear that others have seen through their woundedness to the true beauty of their essence. They hear others say things like, "You have a lot of integrity." "I love your intensity and passion." "You are very sweet and gentle, and you have a lot of courage." "I so appreciate the depth of your compassion and empathy." "You have a healing touch." Hearing these things one after another from a group of people who have just witnessed all your anger, fear, and pain is a powerful experience. It is very healing to be seen for who we really are underneath our fear-driven controlling behavior.

Elisha was brought up in a family where she was often shamed by her parents. They told her she was ugly, stupid, and good for nothing. When Elisha excelled, her parents diminished her achievements by comparing her to someone else more successful. They never encouraged her or supported her in any way. They never reflected her wonderful qualities to her.

At one of my intensives, Elisha worked hard on facing and healing her wounds. She was courageous in her willingness to face her fear and pain. She was also brilliant, perceptive, and talented. She paid close attention when others worked and offered her support during the whole five days. Everyone fell in love with Elisha, not because of her outer attractiveness, but because of the light that shone from within.

Yet before the intensive, Elisha had not thought much of herself. She still carried her parents' view of her. No matter how much she accomplished in the external world, she could not get beyond their cruel distortions of her worth.

At the intensive, Elisha became connected with her spiritual guidance. Through its eyes, she began to experience a true view of herself. By the end of our five days together, Elisha was able to take it in when people mirrored her core self to her, telling her about her inner light, her compassion, perceptiveness, gentleness, intelligence, creativity, and courage. Tears of joy streaked Elisha's face as one by one we held up a loving mirror for her.

Rick, a very intense young film director, was brought up in a quiet, sedate family. From childhood he had been told that he was too intense, so he had spent enormous energy containing his excitement, joy, passion, and sense of wonder—as well as his intense loneliness and heartbreak. All that remained was his intense anger, which he often released on those around him.

Throughout his five-day intensive, Rick's intensity was met with total acceptance. Everyone loved the passion with which he expressed himself. Instead of being threatened by it, as his parents were, we felt blessed by it. At the end, when we offered Rick the gift of mirroring, many of us expressed how much we loved his intensity. He was deeply moved and said that he had never experienced this level of safety and acceptance before in his life.

We cannot change people's negative view of themselves: they have to be open to their own guidance to see their shining truth, but we can support them by mirroring their essence. When we do this for each other, we strengthen the safe relationship space between us.

When couples first come to see me, they usually have a distorted view of each other—seeing each other primarily as their wounded self. They lose sight of their partner's wonderful core self because they do not know their own true self. As they practice Inner Bonding and learn to see their own essence, their eyes are opened to their partner's essence. I have often had the incredibly moving experience of hearing one partner mirror for the other who they see them to be. Many times, the qualities they formerly found threatening—such as intensity, sensitivity, perceptiveness, or passion—are the ones they now value, as well as the very ones they fell in love with.

I have found that the more we value ourselves, the more the people in our lives value us. The world seems to mirror our own inner system. When we judge and reject ourselves, we may feel judged and rejected by others. When we disrespect ourselves, we may be disrespected. When we ignore ourselves, we might be ignored. When we value ourselves, the people in our world may mirror that value back to us.

There are wonderful opportunities to mirror each other in relationships with partners, friends, family members, and coworkers. The more time we spend sharing who we really are with each other, the more opportunities we have to see each other's essence. However, we can even offer mirroring in a brief encounter, say with a kind store clerk, by letting the person know we appreciate their kindness. Holding up a loving mirror for one another, friends and strangers alike, is a profound way to allow God to work through us.

Being in the Moment

The wounded self spends its time ruminating about the past and fantasizing about the future. But the past is gone and the future has not yet happened. The only reality is the present moment. The loving adult lives in the moment. Only by being in the moment can you be aware of your inner experience, your spiritual guidance, and your experience of the world. This is why Step One of Inner Bonding is being mindful of your inner experience in the moment. You cannot do the six steps of Inner Bonding unless you are present in this moment.

When you assume that what happened to you in the past is also happening in the present and will happen in the future, you are no longer operating in reality. For example, if a man was rejected as a boy by his father, he may assume (consciously or unconsciously) that everyone will treat him as his father did. You cannot create a safe inner space or a safe relationship space when you are projecting your old fears and beliefs onto the present and future. When you are not operating in the reality of this moment, you may protect yourself against a perceived present or future threat with unloving, controlling behavior.

Many people spend years in therapy trying to remember and understand the past, but I have found this to be fairly useless. *The present illumi-*

nates the past: you don't have to search for it. When you are practicing Inner Bonding and exploring your present-day fears and false beliefs, the process will naturally reveal the past: it's where you first acquired these fears and beliefs. The more you are in the moment, noticing your feelings and behavior, and embracing your inner child whenever you feel anything less than peaceful and full inside, the more you will remember, understand, heal, and move beyond your wounded past.

The wounded self is addicted to thinking about the past and the future. We delude ourselves into believing that if we think enough about the past and the future, we can control the present and therefore the outcomes of things. As long as our intent is to control, our programmed mind will remain addicted to ruminating about the past and the future.

Only when you choose the intent to learn about loving yourself will you move out of your programmed, wounded mind into your open, receptive mind and into being present in your body—into the real experience of the moment. When you, as a loving adult, open your heart and embrace your inner experience, you will always be guided toward your highest good. Once you experience this ever-present guidance, you will know that there is no point in ruminating about the past or worrying about the future.

As you practice Inner Bonding and learn to be present in the moment, you will discover that your thoughts come from your spiritual guidance rather than from your programmed, wounded self. These thoughts come from truth rather than from false beliefs, and they bring peace rather than stress.

Courage

It takes courage to speak your truth without blame or judgment, to stay open to learning despite your fears, and to disengage in the face of your partner's closed or violating behavior. It takes courage to love yourself enough to do the difficult things. Actually, this is the definition of courage: loving yourself or others enough to take loving action even when it is scary. Courage is an essential ingredient in creating a safe relationship space.

I have known people whose fear is so great that they would rather parachute into the middle of a war zone than allow themselves to open up and become vulnerable to their core pain in a relationship. Statistics tell us that human beings fear public speaking more than death. This is because it puts us at great risk of disapproval and rejection and feeling the loneliness and heartbreak that we work so hard to avoid. Since our deepest fears of rejection arise in love relationships, I wonder if there aren't more people willing to speak in public than to be truly open and vulnerable with a loved one, especially when there is conflict.

How many of us have the courage to become strong enough to love? When we do summon that courage and do our inner work, the rewards are many.

Rewards of Becoming Strong Enough to Love

Practicing Inner Bonding allows you to keep your heart open in the face of fear. Instead of being a victim of others' choices (or of your own false beliefs), you can choose who you want to be in each and every moment.

When you can keep your heart open, you are free to give and receive love. All the energy you previously spent proving your worth and avoiding your core painful feelings can now go into joyfully expressing yourself. As you heal the layers of your wounded self and discover the beauty of your core self, the blueprint of why you came to this planet emerges, and you discover your passion, your purpose, and your true work. Life becomes a lot more fun!

Inner Bonding gives you the tools and self-discipline to move beyond your addictions, since you no longer need to fill yourself from the outside. Anger becomes a manageable feeling, a signal that your inner child needs your attention rather than an expression of blame or violence. Patience replaces irritation. Procrastination and other forms of resistance become a thing of the past. You learn to speak your truth rather than taking rejection personally or losing yourself in the face of others' controlling behavior, and to move through core pain. You become a powerful and peaceful person.

Rewards of Creating a Safe Relationship Spac

A safe relationship space is the fertile soil that nurtures the joyful expression of self. This sacred space provides an arena in which each partner can heal, learn, and grow into the fullness of their being.

Healthy Relationships, Healthy Families

It should be obvious by now that if we each did our inner work, the divorce rate would go way down, and families would not be broken up. Love relationships and families would become joyful learning environments, where each person can heal from past hurts and is supported in being all they can be.

If we healed our own wounds, the deep wounding of children would simply stop. As we each learned to be consistently loving, we would experience a continuity of caring in our relationships that would give us a deep sense of safety. Instead of a burden, life would become a pleasure and a sacred privilege. Laughter, joy, and, creativity would be the norm, not anxiety and depression.

Our planet is not a safe place for most people. They feel unsafe not only at home, but at school, at work, in their cars, in public places, or just out taking a walk. Acting from our wounded selves, we have managed to make our world an unsafe space. This lack of safety starts in the home, continues in schools, and extends to the workplace. People who feel safe and respected are far less likely to act out with alcohol, drugs, and violence than people who are overloaded with fear and rage.

Healing our society starts with healing ourselves and our relationships. Parents who first do their inner work to create a safe inner space and then do the work to create a safe relationship space, will create a safe family space for their children. Children who grow up feeling safe, loved, and respected will bring their experience into the workplace, into government, and into their everyday interactions.

Each of us can contribute to the peace of this beautiful planet by doing our inner work and becoming powerful, loving human beings. How different would life be if we stopped judging ourselves and others, if we stopped taking others' behavior personally, and if we stopped trying to control others and the outcome of things! Imagine how wonderful life would be here on our beautiful Mother Earth if each of us were to take full personal responsibility for our own feelings and behavior, moving beyond the greed that comes from the inner emptiness of self-abandonment and becoming strong enough to love.

Enhanced Physical Health

Our physical health improves when our home and work environments feel safe. Our immune systems are enhanced by the release of loving and creative energy.

It is well documented that people who love their work and feel respected take far fewer sick days. The

January 1999 issue of the *American Journal of Health Promotion* featured a rigorous three-year workplace study that named stress and depression as the leading risk factors for today's employees. Surprisingly, the study found that stress and depression have substantially more impact on physical health than smoking, hypertension, or obesity. Unscheduled absences from work due to stress doubled in just two years, from 1995 to 1997. In addition, half of the employees participating in this study admitted to unethical or illegal activities, and blamed them on job-related stress.

Studies from eleven years ago estimated that "U.S. workplaces lose 172 million work days yearly to depression,"* and the annual cost of stress and depression at the workplace in 2010 was estimated to be $210.5 billion a year and rising. Depression and stress in the workplace affects almost one in every 10 U.S. adults. Not only does it cost workers their jobs, it causes physical illnesses such as heart attacks and strokes. Studies show that the correlation between these illnesses and stress and depression runs as high as 90 percent.

Just as it is personally rewarding to create a safe relationship space, it would certainly pay corporations to create safe, respectful workspaces. "According to the Centers for Disease Control and

---

* Emily A. Kuhl, "Quantifying the Cost of Depression," Workplace Mental Health website, accessed Dec. 10, 2021: https://www.workplacementalhealth. org/mental-health-topics/depression/quantifying-the-cost-of-depression.

Prevention (CDC), productivity losses related to personal and family health problems cost U.S. employers $1,685 per employee per year, or $225.8 billion annually."[*] These figures do not include the less obvious costs due to diminished motivation, lost innovation, and increased errors due to depression and illness. All this will change when we each learn to create internal and external safety, whether we are at work or at home.

Creativity at Home and at Work

A safe space is a creative space, a space that fosters learning, growth, and the discovery of passion and purpose. A safe inner space is the foundation that allows a safe relationship space to develop and magnify creative possibilities. When two or more people are gathered to learn, they generate far more creative power than one can achieve alone. Each person's ideas generate more ideas as the creative energy swirls around, imbuing all with an awesome creative power.

My friend Donna Shirley, who worked with Inner Bonding for years, was an engineer at Jet Propulsion Labs (JPL), which managed the Mars Exploration Program. She was the original leader of the team that built the Sojourner Rover, which enthralled the

---

[*] "Five Reasons Employee Wellness Is Worth the Investment," Creating Healthy Cultures at Work (website), Nov. 6, 2017: https://www.mymedwellness.com/Medwell_blog/2017/11/06/five-reasons-employee-wellness-is-worth-the-investment/.

world when it landed on Mars on July 4, 1997, along with the Mars Pathfinder. Donna is also the author of *Managing Martians* and *Managing Creativity*. She is an expert on creating safe relationship spaces that foster high creativity and productivity.

In *Managing Creativity*, Donna says, "Creativity is generally viewed as an individual pursuit, and, of course, it can be, but groups can produce things that one person can hardly imagine. Spacecraft, cathedrals, good schools, parks, medicines, and computers all result from group or 'collective' creativity."

Donna believes we need "cooperative processes" to establish the environment for creativity. "The challenge is to make it more productive, more congenial, and more fun.... Creative endeavors should be fun, exciting, stimulating, and allow for personal expression, but they must also produce something that will work and sell."

This kind of "fun, exciting, stimulating" creativity can blossom in both home and work environments. In a cooperative, creative environment, chores or duties no longer need be drudgery. Instead of being relegated to off-hours, fun becomes an integral part of the safe relationship space.

When an enlightened manager such as Donna creates a safe, open learning environment instead of a controlling one, not only is creativity heightened, so is productivity. Not only are people more productive, but their work is of higher quality. When people operate from fear of disapproval, they try to do things right to gain approval instead of as an expression of their natural desire to be competent. Competence comes from the inner desire to express ourselves in whatever way is available. The rampant incompetence in our work force results from a lack of caring about the quality of work. People who fear engulfment and resist control by those in authority may do as little work as they can. Others, motivated by a desire to gain approval and avoid disapproval, may do much more work than is necessary and end up exhausted. In an effort to gain approval, they may do things right, but their creativity may fall by the wayside in their efforts to prove themselves rather than express themselves.

As Donna points out, "Organizations are going to have to change their practices in order to take full advantage of the creativity of their people.... In a balanced state, discomfort gives way to excitement and determination. Anxiety is transformed into energy, as the creativity of the group is focused on getting a job done. In this state, desired results are not only possible, they call forth the best efforts that often attain greatness."

When we desire to express ourselves rather than prove ourselves, we don't compete; we cooperate and support each other. When we desire to be our best rather than being better than others, competition simply doesn't exist. In a safe relationship space, even sibling relationships become cooperative instead of competitive.

Inner Peace and Joy

Joy is the incredible feeling of fullness and well-being, the deep happiness, that comes from connecting with yourself, with your spiritual guidance, and with others. Most of us have had moments of joy that occur spontaneously. Through practicing Inner Bonding and becoming strong enough to love, you can have more and more joy and inner peace in your life. They are the rewards of creating a safe inner space and a safe relationship space!

Your joy is the most important thing you can offer to the planet. Doing your inner work not only affects your own personal well-being, but affects the well-being of our entire planet. Imagine what our world would be like if everyone took responsibility for their own joy!

8

Creating Safe Living and Learning Spaces for Our Children

When children grow up in controlling, unsafe relationship spaces, they learn to be controlling too. The rise in adolescent violence in our schools attests to the fact that these teens, apparently suffering from rejection both at home and at school, with no role models for being a loving adult, have developed no loving inner adult to set limits on their behavior and manage their feelings.

We can continue to form organizations to help children like this, but these measures are only Band-Aids. The problem, like all the other problems in our society, needs to be resolved on the level of intent.

Loving adults, connected with their own essence, physically and emotionally nurture the beautiful essences of their children. They treat their children, from infancy on, as the sacred beings they are—with kindness, warmth, caring, and respect. A loving adult with the ability to set appropriate inner limits could never physically or sexually act out on a child. It is time to recognize that healing is necessary and possible, and that money needs to be spent on healing.

The social costs of child abuse are enormous. Prison inmate profiles are rife with histories of childhood abuse. Without a process such as Inner Bonding to turn to in times of stress, parents resort to acting out on their children, perpetuating the very experiences from their own childhood that may be causing their stress.

When our children do not receive the love and role modeling they need to fill themselves spiritually instead of with substances, they are very vulnerable to the drug scene. Too many of our nation's youth are at risk of damaging their lives through harmful behavior for lack of family, school, and community efforts to nurture young adolescents. The costs to our society are enormous in terms of crime, violence, alienation, hatred, ignorance, incompetence, disease, disability, and suicide. The solution is to provide young people with close relationships with loving and dependable adults who are capable of role modeling personal responsibility for their own feeling and behavior. But where are these loving and dependable adults? Without a process such as Inner Bonding being taught in schools (we are offering our online program, SelfQuest®, which teaches Inner Bonding, to both prisons and high schools), there are not enough children growing up into loving and dependable adults to provide the necessary nurturing and role modeling for their own children.

A number of years ago, I was a speaker at a national drug conference for parents, educators, therapists, and teenagers. I was in the speakers' lounge waiting for my turn when a man came in to register as a speaker. He had his little daughter with him, an adorable and precocious three-year-old who was asking a lot of questions. He turned to her and said, "Be still or I will whip you!" I sat there stunned, wondering how he could possibly show parents and educators how to help troubled youth when he was doing his best to create a troubled daughter.

The little girl then asked for water, and he said to her in a shaming voice, "No, it will make you go to the bathroom," as if going to the bathroom were a shameful thing to do. This man just couldn't be bothered with his three-year-old daughter's natural needs.

I motioned for the child to come over to me, and I asked the father if I could take her to get water. He said, "OK, but not too much."

When we came back, he said to her accusingly, "Did you drink too much?"

She looked up at me with big, frightened eyes, and asked, "Did I?"

"No," I replied.

Then she came over to me, sat on my lap, and said through tears of heartbreak, "I don't like my daddy. He's mean. I will never like him. Do you have a daddy?"

"Yes," I answered, choking back my own tears that this precious child was already so frightened of her daddy and already felt so unsafe. "Is he mean?" she asked.

"Not very often," I said.

"Mine is."

"Yes, he is," I agreed. At least I could validate her experience. "And you are a very sweet little girl," I said, and I hugged her.

Her father then called her, and as she clung to me for a moment, I felt my heart break for her. When she walked over to her father, someone else in the room said, "She's cute."

"Yeah," he answered, "but all she does is eat, drink water, and go to the bathroom."

After the man left, I went to the speaker's desk to find out who he was, but the woman there couldn't remember. "Did you see how he treated his daughter?" I asked.

"No," she said. "I didn't notice."

She didn't notice! How could she not notice! She was working at a conference of people who are supposed to notice! At that moment I felt very discouraged about our society.

With the breakdown of the family, children often join gangs to feel a sense of belonging. Without parents who are personally responsible and care about their children, children look for a sense of identity outside of the family. Their deep loneliness makes them vulnerable to gangs, just as people who are spiritually disconnected and yearn to belong are vulnerable to cults. Our families will continue to break down until people practice Inner Bonding. A safe planet comes from safe families, and safe families come from safe, open, and loving individuals.

Trust-Level Communication to Create Safe Learning Spaces

We have lost our way when it comes to educating our children. We are so locked into tests and grades that we have forgotten all about the true joy of learning. Many of our children hate school, and this is very sad. A part of our crime problem is related to our poor educational system: school is so boring that too many teenagers drop out and turn to the streets, selling drugs, and committing crimes, or turn to online scamming. With the mass shootings at schools, some adolescents drop out because school is such an unsafe place to be. In the light of COVID, many children and adolescents are relieved when they don't have to go to in-person school.

Many of our teachers are wounded people whose unhealed need for control is acted out upon the students, disempowering and humiliating them. Many of us have emotional scars related to the rejection and humiliation suffered at school. Often classrooms are places of fear instead of safety, and children cannot learn when they are afraid. School also is the arena where bullies act out the woundedness created by their unsafe home environments. The violence in our schools attests to the great need for healing in our society.

My friend Olivia Douglas, a past educator in Bremen, Germany, who embraced Inner Bonding, developed a method of teaching she called TLC: Trust-Level Communication. For many years, she taught junior high and high school problem children, some of whom had backgrounds in crime. Many of her students came from different countries and did not know the language when they began her class. Olivia had enormous success with her caring methods. Very few of her students dropped out, and 95 percent of her graduates went on to jobs or job training. She managed to create a sense of community, trust, and caring among her students. She could even leave her purse out, and no student would take anything from her. She had the same class for six years, which gave her the time she needed to create community and instill spiritual values. She incorporated Inner Bonding into her teaching. The following is a brief outline, written by Olivia, of her aims and methods. The aims of TLC are:

- To enable students to organize themselves.
- To learn to work in groups together.
- To know how to get the information needed for a project.
- To cope with both dominant and nondominant coworkers.

- To integrate with people of different races, religions, abilities, and opinions.
- To have discussions over different points of view with the aim to learn.
- To create a nonviolent atmosphere.
- To be able to handle addictions.
- To be able to judge their work themselves.

The methods to reach these goals are:
- Establishing trust by being trustworthy, consistent with caring and boundaries.
- Teaching in groups that stay together from grades 7 through 12.
- Teaching in projects.
- There are no teachers, only helpers.
- A step-by-step withdrawal of the helper's activities until they are not needed.
- Participants learn how to judge their work through a question system.
- A flexible time schedule while maintaining the integrity of the group.
- Few different helpers.
- No pressure on the students. It is their choice to work or not to work.
- Full acceptance of everyone, even the nonworkers.
- The helpers have no right to say, "I know what's good for you."
- The first steps are the basic skills, which are brought in by the helpers.

- Craftsman skills and abstract themes are balanced equally.
- Everyday skills are offered, like household skills, filling in forms, going to officials, applying for jobs, and dealing with money.
- Theme projects are brought in by everyone on a democratic basis.
- Dealing actively and openly with group problems.
- Taking time to talk over personal problems.
- Growing into caring for themselves, for others, and for the environment.
- Help through Inner Bonding.
- Help through learning about nutrition.
- Doing things just for fun, motivation, and self-confidence.

The following is a report she wrote to me about her teaching:

The basic idea is that all persons, no matter what age, are able to decide for themselves what their task is.

The role of teacher or parent is to provide an atmosphere in which the child or adolescent is able to discover what they want to do. When power struggles exist, this cannot happen. It is up to the teacher or parent to act out of love, and not out of fear—to be Inner Bonded. Then actions geared to establish power are not necessary, and the kids do not feel the need to oppose or resist.

This might sound easy, and convincing in theory, but how do you put it into practice? Letting the kids do whatever they want? Allowing complete chaos? We have heard of this before: anti-authoritarian education!

No, that's not what this is all about. The basic concept is that students can certainly decide for themselves, but "your freedom ends where the other person's nose begins." The teacher or parent intervenes when one person intrudes on the space of another. No one has the right to do that.

But what happens when, during an English lesson, Walter is drawing little pictures into his exercise book instead of doing English? He is not disturbing anyone else. Well, I go to him, and I ask whether he has made a clear decision to draw instead of learn English. This is the point where you cannot lie as a teacher. If you are Inner Bonded, your inner attitude to Walt is that you trust him to make the right decision for himself. He feels trust coming towards him, not fear. This might take time, perhaps two years, before a class has the bonded atmosphere.

Until then, Walt might have drawn many little pictures to find out whether the pictures or the English are more important for what he wants to do in his life. We all know what was more important to Walt Disney in the end, though his teachers did not have any trust in his little pictures.

We cannot know what is right for another person. We do not know the other person's path or task. That's why we need to respect a student's decision without expectations or judgment.

Sometimes parents or colleagues are troubled by what I'm doing. Most of the time they accept it in the end because they see violent pupils calming down and insecure pupils becoming more self-confident.

The other day a former pupil came to see me at home, and he told me that at the company where he works, he is the only apprentice who is respected rather than yelled at. He explained that after the first time he was yelled at, he went to his boss and admitted that what he did was wrong and that he would make it right, but that this was no reason to despise or degrade him. He told the boss that if he knew how to do everything right, he would not be an apprentice. His boss was so impressed that ever since, he would tell him how to do things rather than yelling at him. This former pupil now had the self-confidence and calmness to set good boundaries, but when he came into my class years ago, he smashed a door in when he didn't like what I said to him.

When you start, the number of washbasins ripped out of the wall or doors smashed in is only slowly reduced, because all the frustration of the past years sometimes has to spill out before other feelings can start to feel at home. Starting with a new class is very hard, especially with lower grade classes in poor areas.

So what makes John express himself with his mouth instead of his fist? For some time, I offer to be the door he wants to smash in. He starts hitting, and he finds it—open. This is quite a shock. So he tries again, and again, until he doesn't feel like it anymore.

Example: During a lesson John starts kicking his table, and is obviously in a rage over something. I go to him and ask him what's wrong. He is not talking to me. He just says things like, "It's always the same. I'm fed up with that kind of bullshit. You teachers are all the same."

I say, "OK, tell me what's wrong."

He just keeps kicking the table.

I ask, "What has the table done to you?"

"What, the table? Nothing!"

"So who has done something to you?"

"You."

"So tell me what I have done wrong—not the table."

"Ah, there is no use. All I get is trouble if I say so, and you don't change a damn thing."

"Try me."

By then, others urge him to speak. "Tell her what you say to us!"

So he starts. "OK, you're real mean. You don't like me. You never ask me when I want to say something. You don't give me a chance. You have those you like, and they are always asked."

I stand there completely baffled. I turn to the rest of the class. "Do you think so too?"

Some turn away, some start shouting at me. "Yes, and there you did . . . and there you didn't . . ." After a while, I say, "Stop! Let's talk about it in a way that I cannot refuse to hear you. As long as you are shouting at me, it is hard to listen to you."

I ask one of the boys to be the director. He is in charge of the speakers list. I only speak when it is my turn. This is quite a new experience for the kids. It's not me and them anymore. Everyone has the same right to speak. Now they tell me that I am mean, bad, and so on, because this kid is not treated in the same way as the others. They give examples where I have taken too little notice of him.

First, I listen. Then I ask if others have seen the same. If so, I ask them what they think that I should do differently. They say that I should take as much or as little notice of him as of others. I say that they should help me. If they think that I am leaving him out, they should tell me so. Then we work out how this can be done. I say to them, "If you just insult me, I can't take you very seriously. I won't listen to you. Why should I? Would you?"

"No, never!"

"Well, if you shout at me, 'You're so mean,' I can easily turn away, and not take seriously what you say. But if you come to me and say, 'Excuse, please, but I would like to talk to you. I think what you did was unjust because . . .' I can turn away once maybe, but after some time I will have to listen to you, because there is no reason left to object to it."

We role-play the situation in different versions. Then it is quite clear how to do it. They find that it is very important to define clearly what they want to say to avoid misunderstandings. Sometimes they say, "But you know what I mean."

"Then say it."

"But how?"

So we change roles. I give them the reasons they should tell me, so that I have to accept it. After some time, this technique works very well. It becomes a kind of game. They tell each other or me how to say things better, in a more precise way.

After some practice, this technique is used with other teachers or adults. They are not always pleased about it at first, but in the end, it usually works out very well. It depends on the amount of fear a teacher has about losing power over the kids. They may project this fear onto you if it is so intense that they cannot cope with it. Under normal circumstances, these adults will in the end understand what has happened and accept it or even go into the whole Inner Bonding process themselves. No further help will be required then.

"So you let them do anything they like? They are always getting their own way?" No, of course not. We are all setting clear boundaries. This has to be respected.

Learning to establish and respect boundaries is a vital part of the process we go through together. If I am in a situation where I feel it is going too far, I will set the boundary, and so will the kids.

This learning has an effect on many other people in the child's life. For example, Mary was constantly beaten up by her mother's boyfriend. When he is drunk, he beats her mother too. Mary rejected any relationship that lasted longer than an evening. After two years of going through the Inner Bonding process at school, she was not beaten up anymore by this boyfriend, and was going out normally. She even sent her mother to talk with me. Her mother did, but did not continue, although she admired how her daughter was coping. But at least she managed then to stop the boyfriend from beating her. Even years after leaving school, Mary and I are still in contact. She is trying to get her mother to start the Inner Bonding process.

Others come with their partners and want to talk about Inner Bonding. So the effect is lasting even after schooltime—maybe even a lifetime.

When I was in Germany, teaching an Inner Bonding workshop, I met Olivia's class and was greatly impressed by their level of caring about each other and their understanding of Inner Bonding. Olivia showed me one of their projects: constructing a bicycle. They bought old parts and put together the bicycles. The students had to learn about mechanics, balance, and so on. Once the bikes were complete, they sold them. They learned about selling and profit. Then, as a group, they decided what to do with their profit. They decided to paint a huge mural on one of their high walls. They learned about design, color, spatial relationships, and perspective. The mural is an incredible work of art, and the students got to see it daily, reminding them of their accomplishments.

Education can be a joy. Schools can become safe places where each individual child's soul is allowed to blossom in its own unique way, where creativity and passion for learning are fostered.

It all comes down to intent. When each of us embraces the intent to learn and becomes strong enough to love, our homes, schools, and work environments will become places of caring and respect. Let's each do our part in creating a safe planet.

Epilogue
Going One Step Further: Creating a Safe Planet

Creating a safe planet is an extension of creating a safe relationship space. Both result from choosing to be on the spiritual path of the intent to learn about love rather than the earthly path of the intent to control.

When we operate from the intent to control and define ourselves externally rather than internally, we believe that we will not be OK if we lose something or don't get what we want. Often our wanting gets in the way of our caring. When we want something—love, money, power, pleasure, safety, or the avoidance of pain—we may not look at the consequences of our desires: Who suffers when we get what we want? When our motive is power over others, we do not consider the costs. We ignore the consequences our choices have on others. This not only affects us on a personal and family level, but on a global level.

Many aspects of our government, most of our educational institutions, numerous religious organizations, and many couples, and families are devoted to control rather than to love. When we are devoted to power over others instead of power within, we can do untold harm to each other through violence, crime, sexism, and racism. Earthly values and the resulting desire for control lead us to divide and stand against each other, rather than uniting for the highest good of each of us and experiencing the oneness that we feel when we know our own beautiful essence. Then we can see and value the beautiful essence in each of us.

Our society is rampant with individuals, businesses, and organizations who operate from earthly values, particularly concerning money. To the wounded self, money is generally synonymous with worth. In our society, people who are financially wealthy are considered more important and valuable than those without it. Social stature is measured by wealth, fame, and good looks rather than by integrity, kindness, caring, honesty, commitment, and goodness.

Because money can give us power over others, it is a major form of control in our culture. Money puts political leaders into power. The person who controls the money in a family usually controls the family. In fact, money causes more arguments than any other family issue.

Too often the power and control that comes with making a lot of money is more important than caring about the welfare of others or the environment. *The greed of the wounded self is destroying our planet.* Indigenous peoples lived on Mother Earth for thousands of years without taking or destroying anything. But we, as a "civilized" society, are rapidly destroying the land that feeds us—all because of the intent to control and the resulting greed and lack of caring. To the wounded self, the means justifies the end. Wounded people who crave money, power, and control put no limits on what they will do to others, the soil that feeds us, and the environment and ecosystems that sustain us, to make the money that will give them the power they desire.

How wonderful it would be if more wealthy people saw themselves as blessed with money in order to be warriors of love on the planet! If the wealthy define their worth and lovability through how much they help others instead of through the price of their houses, cars, and yachts (and flying rich and privileged individuals into space), our world will become a safer, more loving place. What if these people spent their billions on ending hunger and climate change, and bringing our planet back into balance?

Many businesses, especially big business, focus solely on profits. Granted, it is more challenging to manage from ethics and integrity than to simply manage for profits. When you manage for profits, you manage for tangibles: time, space, efficiency. The human spirit and the safe relationship space are not figured into the equation. Managing for profits does not take into account the common good. Until businesses recognize that caring about the common good is essential to our survival, profit will remain their god.

Big businesses that make spiritual values as important as profit have a huge impact on bettering our society. Fortunately, some businesses are recognizing the power they have to support the common good.

Big corporations have, for the most part, shied away from seminars that teach a "soft" approach such as Inner Bonding. They are still focused primarily on learning things that will raise their profits and give them more control. Until the CEOs themselves recognize that they, like each of us, are responsible for what is happening to this planet, things will not change. In fact, people who wield power have an even greater responsibility, since what they do affects so many people. If the CEOs of the Fortune 500 businesses decided to operate from spiritual values, learned Inner Bonding themselves, and offered their employees our patented SelfQuest online program to learn Inner Bonding, they could change the world.

If we learned to be loving adults in our homes, schools, and churches, we would each be taking personal responsibility for ourselves while caring about the needs of others. We desperately need to build Inner Bonding into our society so that we can all move toward becoming personally responsible and compassionate human beings. Our problems of poverty, homelessness, crime, racism, sexism, education, and health care could be resolved if we had enough compassionate people who cared about the common good and experienced our oneness with all living beings, including Mother Earth, and put their time into solving these problems.

We don't require our leaders to do the personal healing they need to do to become honest and trustworthy. Training in interpersonal relationships is not required of candidates running for office. In fact, just as there is no training required to be a parent, there is no training required to be president: all it takes is enough money, enough powerful people, and, until 2012, being a white male.

Money is power. We can stay locked into earthly values and use the power of money to control, or we can do our inner work, becoming loving adults who operate from spiritual values, and use the power of money to support the common good.

Spiritual values are based on experiencing that we are one and that if we harm another, we harm ourselves. When we are connected to the spiritual realm, we know that every act, beneficial or harmful, has a ripple effect, affecting every other soul, since on the spiritual level we are each a part of the whole, a part of the unconditional love that is God.

When we operate from spiritual values, we have a deep reverence for all of life. We cannot purposely do harm to others or to the planet. When operating on the earthly level, it's each person for themselves, but on the spiritual level, we are devoted to the common good. We see all of life the same way we see our own bodies: if we harm one cell, we harm the whole. On the spiritual level, we recognize that we cannot violate others in any way—physically, emotionally, psychically, financially, or spiritually—without violating ourselves. Our soul is love, and when we violate others in any way, we violate our own soul. When we recognize this truth, we will stop hurting each other and instead strive for our own and one another's highest good.

We each have the choice to operate from earthly values or spiritual values. Our survival and the survival of our planet depends upon choosing spiritual values.

Resources

These resources are available at innerbonding.com. You can also find information on Events, including Intensives and support groups; Inner Bonding Village (a compassionate membership community); and Facilitators and Facilitator Training.

Books

Healing Your Aloneness, 1990
The first book written on Inner Bonding. Takes you on a deep inner journey of healing. Helps you understand who the Child is, who the loving Adult is, and how to dialogue. Lots of examples.

Inner Bonding, 1992
Inner Bonding becomes a five step process in this next book. This book presents role modeling regarding how to take loving care of yourself in your relationships with your mate, friends, parents, children, and co-workers.

The Healing Your Aloneness Workbook, 1993
Teaches the Six Steps of Inner Bonding through many different exercises.

Do I Have To Give Up Me To Be Loved By God?, 1999
This book helps you heal any problems you have in your relationship with your Higher Power. It goes more deeply into the Inner Bonding process and teaches you how to have a direct, personal relationship with Divine Guidance—a relationship that heals emptiness, relationship problems, addictions, and leads to personal empowerment.

Do I Have To Give Up Me To Be Loved By You?, 1983
Describes how the intent to learn, as opposed to the intent to protect, leads to loving conflict resolution in committed relationships, and how conflict becomes the arena for creating learning, growth and passion.

Do I Have To Give Up Me To Be Loved By My Kids?, 1985
Shows how to move beyond authoritarian and permissive parenting into loving parenting from an intent to learn.

Do I Have To Give Up Me To Be Loved By You? . . . The Workbook, 1987
Helps you to discover the ways you protect against the pain you fear that actually creates your present pain.

Diet For Divine Connection: Beyond Junk Foods and Junk Thought To At-Will Divine Connection, 2018
Discover how to experience a consistent, at-will connection with your spiritual source of love and guidance

The Inner Bonding Workbook: Six Steps to Healing Yourself and Connecting with Your Divine Guidance, 2019
A complete experience in learning and deepening your application of Inner Bonding to individual and relationship issues

The Inner Bonding Workbook: Six Steps to Healing Yourself and Connecting with Your Divine Guidance, 2019
A complete experience in learning and deepening your application of Inner Bonding to individual and relationship issues

Six Steps to Total Self-Healing: The Inner Bonding Process, 2021
This book is a transcription of the Inner Bonding Weekend Workshop, with many examples of Dr. Paul working with participants and answering questions.

Audio Tapes
Beyond Fear and Addictions
In this two hour tape set, I present an overview of Inner Bonding, bring you through the Six Steps in a visualization—including contacting your spiritual Guidance—and then I demonstrate the process

with a volunteer from the audience. Questions and answers follow the demo.

Anger and Inner Bonding

In this tape I give a one hour overview of Inner Bonding where the Six Steps are acted out along with the three-part anger process that is part of Step Two.

Opening to Learning Meditation Tape

This is the 20 minute clearing and prayer that I do at the beginning of each day at an intensive. Each intensive participant receives one of these at the end of the intensive.

Do I Have To Give Up Me To Be Loved By Kids?

In this two-hour, 20 minutes set of tapes, we present how to parent children with an intent to learn and role play many different conflict situations, followed by questions and answers.

From Conflict to Intimacy and Beyond

This three-hour tape is exceptionally helpful in teaching the difference between the intent to protect and the intent to learn in conflicts in relationships. Much role playing different conflict situations.

Video Tapes

The Inner Bonding Introductory Lecture
This is a two-hour overview of Inner Bonding, along with the LifePaths charts. Extremely helpful to reminding you of the process and to introducing others to Inner Bonding.

The Master Teacher Connection
In this one hour and 45 minute tape, Erika describes how she sees the spiritual Master Teachers and some of what she has learned from her Teacher. Erika is an excellent speaker and this is a fascinating tape.

Courses

SelfQuest®
SelfQuest is a self-guided journey that takes place at your own pace, in the privacy of your own space. There will be challenges on this journey, but it is a journey well worth the effort because its invaluable rewards will last a lifetime. SelfQuest is a comprehensive educational, personal empowerment and conflict resolution completely encrypted online program.

Love Yourself: A 30-Day At-Home Inner Bonding Course with Dr. Margaret Paul
The $199 course includes videos and visualizations created just for this course, and a daily article. The $299 course also includes a special forum just for participants, and a weekly group call to get your

questions answered. The call will be recorded so if you can't attend at the time, you will receive a copy of it. For about 15–20 minutes a day, you will learn Inner Bonding.

Unlocking Your Inner Wisdom
This course includes daily videos created just for this course and a daily lesson with an action step. For about 15–20 minutes a day, you can learn to connect with your inner guidance and your higher spiritual guidance, or deepen your current connection, and learn the art of manifestation.

Wildly, Deeply, Joyously In Love
This course includes a ohe-hour overview intro video, thirty 10–15 minute videos created just for this course, and a daily lesson with an action step. For about 20 minutes a day, you can learn how to heal your current relationship or how to create the relationships of your dreams, and you can take as long as you want to go through it. It's powerful for a couple, and for an individual, as it applies to all relationships.

Attracting your Beloved: A 30-Day At-home Experience with Dr. Margaret Paul to Learn How to Attract the Love of your Life
This course includes videos and visualizations created just for this course and a daily lesson. The upgraded course includes a special forum just for participants, and a weekly group call to get your

questions answered. The call will be recorded so if you can't attend at the time, you will receive a copy of it. For about 20 minutes a day, you can learn how to attract the love of your life.

Passionate Purpose, Vibrant Health! A 30-Day at home Experience with Dr. Margaret Paul
This course includes videos and visualizations created just for this course, a daily article, a special forum just for participants, and a weekly group call to get your questions answered. The call will be recorded so if you can't attend at the time, you will receive a copy of it. For about 20 minutes a day, you can learn how access the blueprint for your passionate purpose and achieve the health and well-being to manifest it.

Complete Self Love the Ultimate Collection
In this course you'll get a master-level instruction on Inner Bonding, what it is, how to do it, and interactive tools that will help you apply this process in your everyday life to develop self-love.

The Power to Heal Yourself
Free Webinar with Dr. Margaret Paul. Includes a special package called *The Power to Heal Yourself*

The Intimate Relationship Toolbox
This 12-week home-study course, which includes videos, audios and article packets, teaches you the

Steps of Inner Bonding, while also teaching you how to create a loving relationship.

Dr. Margaret's Permanent Weight Loss Course
This 12-week home-study course, which includes videos, audios and article packets, teaches you the Steps of Inner Bonding, while also teaching you how to permanently lose weight.

About the Author

DR. MARGARET PAUL is the cocreator of Inner Bonding®, along with Dr. Erika Chopich, and is author/coauthor of several best-selling books, including *Do I Have to Give Up Me to Be Loved by You?*; *Do I Have to Give Up Me to Be Loved By You?: The Workbook*; *Inner*  *Bonding*; *Healing Your Aloneness*; *The Healing Your Aloneness Workbook*; *Do I Have to Give Up Me to Be Loved by My Kids?*; *Do I Have to Give Up Me to Be Loved by God?*; *Diet for Divine Connection: Beyond Junk Foods and Junk Thoughts to At-Will Spiritual Connection*; *The Inner Bonding Workbook: Six Steps to Healing Yourself and Connecting with Your Divine Guidance*, and *Six Steps to Total Self-Healing: The Inner Bonding Process.*

Dr. Paul's books have been distributed around the world and have been translated into many languages.

She holds a PhD in psychology and is a relationship expert, noted public speaker, workshop leader, educator, consultant, and artist. She has appeared on many radio and TV shows, including *The Oprah Show*. She has successfully worked with tens of thousands of individuals, couples, and business relationships and has taught classes and seminars since 1967.

Margaret continues to work with individuals, couples, and groups throughout the world on the phone, Zoom, and Skype. During her sessions, workshops, and Intensives, she is able to access her own and her clients' spiritual guidance, which enables her to work with people wherever they are in the world. She offers life-changing thirty-day courses, and she continues to conduct One-Day Inner Bonding Breakthroughs, Inner Bonding Workshops and Three-Day and Five-Day Inner Bonding intensives. She continues to develop content for www.innerbonding.com, and her passion is distributing SelfQuest®, the online program that teaches Inner Bonding. It is being offered to prisons and schools and sold to the general public.

In her spare time, Margaret loves to paint, make pottery, read, learn, grow, and spend time with her loved ones.